GROWING
THROUGH
DIVORCE

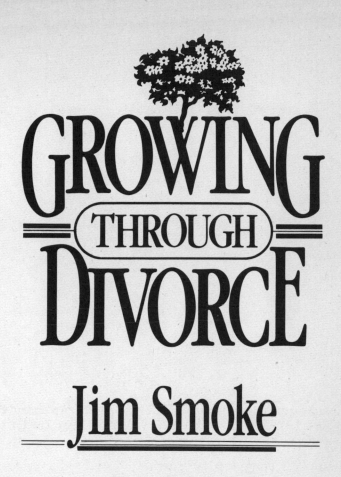

GROWING THROUGH DIVORCE

Jim Smoke

A working guide for *Growing Through Divorce*
is available for individual or group study.

HARVEST HOUSE PUBLISHERS
Eugene, Oregon 97402

Scripture quotations are taken from the New American Standard Bible, and New Testament © 1960, 1962, 1963, 1968, 1971 The Lockman Foundation.

GROWING THROUGH DIVORCE

Copyright © 1976 Harvest House Publishers
Eugene, Oregon 97402
Library of Congress Catalog Card Number: 76-21980
ISBN - 0-89081-081-8

Printed in the United States of America

Dedicated to

THE POSITIVE CHRISTIAN SINGLES

of

GARDEN GROVE COMMUNITY CHURCH

Garden Grove, California

**GROWING
THROUGH
DIVORCE**

INTRODUCTION

Divorce is one of the most painful and emotionally draining experiences that a human being can have. It results in the death of a marriage but does not have the finality of physical death. The vestiges of a former way of life remain to remind and overshadow a present existence. It is a hurt that goes deep and is accompanied by the doubt that it will ever heal.

In a society that has a pill or a prescription for almost everything, very little is being offered to help the person struggling through the hurricane of divorce.

This book comes from a firsthand experience of working with hundreds of formerly married persons; listening to them, struggling with them, caring for them and offering them the choice of either "going through divorce" or "GROWING THROUGH DIVORCE."

Special thanks to the many people I know who are displaying by their life that they are growing through their divorce.

My thanks also to:
- Irene Wallace, my secretary, for her creative support and manuscript typing.
- Dave Stoop, critic, editor and personal friend.
- Dr. Robert H. Schuller, founding pastor of Garden Grove Community Church, for his vision, leadership and Christian love that permits an authentic church ministry to formerly married persons.

Jim Smoke

GROWING
THROUGH
DIVORCE

FOREWORD

One of the deepest wounds that can strike any individual today is divorce. How beautiful that God is always ready to forgive!

I have watched my friend and associate Jim Smoke develop these positive possibility principles that are helping to heal the hurts of hundreds of people every week. I am excited that they are now available for you.

This is a book to give to anyone trapped in the despair of divorce. The power of God can triumph. These positive growth principles really work. Broken lives can be beautiful again.

I know that God can effectively use this book in your life or the life of a loved one.

Robert H. Schuller

GROWING
THROUGH
DIVORCE

CONTENTS

GROWING THROUGH DIVORCE

1

IS THIS REALLY HAPPENING TO ME?

> *"Getting married is like buying a phonograph record: you buy it for what's on one side but you have to take the flip side too."*
>
> *"Getting divorced is like getting the hole in the record!"*

Shocked! Angry! Dazed! Bitter! Empty! Cheated!

These, along with an assortment of other feelings probably describe how many people feel when they separate from a marriage that began with optimism, happiness and hope. A terrible thing that somehow always happened to other people has happened to you. In many instances, there is little preparation for the chaos that you are thrown into both emotionally and physically. Many things that were once taken in stride now become major hazards in daily life. You are in "Divorce Country!" You never planned to be here but you are. It's a strange place with different rules, regulations and road signs. You want it all to change and go away. But it won't!

SHOCK—STAGE ONE

The first emotional state that many people go through in a divorce is shock. Shock is a reaction to the impact that this is really happening to me—not some statistic out there in society but ME.

In a state of shock, people react in many different ways. Some retreat within themselves trying to block out all thoughts of what is happening. They deny it mentally and refuse to talk about it with anyone. They withdraw from friends and social contacts. They may move or change jobs. Retreating sometimes turns into running.

Inward feelings may run the gamut from personal feelings of guilt and failure to the transference of those feelings totally to the other person.

People who go inward in a divorce tend to reject positive help and acceptance from others. Growth in a divorce begins with the admission that this is really happening to me. The first step in dealing with any situation is admitting the situation exists. Denying the divorce will not make it go away. Hiding it from family and friends will not resolve it.

Many people experiencing divorce have shared that enough people have isolated them without them having to impose an inward isolation upon themselves. There is a time, however, to evaluate, think through and reflect upon what is happening to you. This constructive retreat generally happens after the shock state has passed.

In the shock state, others tend to go outside themselves. This is prompted by the need to tell all and to tell everyone. Acceptance of the situation is fended off by the constant replay of all the details, feelings and facts of the divorce. Any ear that will listen becomes a target for the talker.

For the outward person, a frantic social pace often keeps the reality of the situation at arms length. Coming, going and doing become all important. If you are too busy to think, you cannot be hurt by your thoughts. But realities have a way of catching up with you and facing them today will set tomorrow free.

In the shock stage, both the inward and the outward person slowly come to an acceptance of the fact that a relationship that once was vital, important and real has died.

WHAT ABOUT HOPE?

Some people prolong the shock stage by desperately clinging to hope. They live on the hope that they can get back together again and that things will work out to a happy ending. They come to professional counselors with hope in their hearts. They look to God and ministers for miracles. They talk to friends and relatives and ask for help and hope. They often talk to the departed mate about reunion. Many refuse to let hope die and enter into a holding pattern that often lasts for years.

Without hope and optimism, life in general would be as dry as dust. But hope has to be coupled with realism. Realism looks at a situation as it exists, not as you would like it to exist. Realism evaluates a situation honestly based on past and present experience. Here are several questions that will help you sort out hope and reality.

1. *Do Both Parties Really Want The Marriage?*

   If a marriage is in trouble and both parties really want the marriage to succeed, there is a high degree of realistic hope providing they will accept professional help. If one party does not really want the marriage, it will not matter how strongly the other party wants it. Many people have no choice in the matter. If the other person has made the decision and leaves, you are reduced to the decision of waiting and hoping for their return or filing for a divorce.

2. *Will Both Parties Accept Professional Help In Reconciliation For As Long As Is Necessary?*

   One of the questions I frequently ask divorced persons is whether or not they went for help when their marriage was deteriorating. Frequently they reply that they wanted and went for help but the other party felt they did not need it or it was not their problem to resolve. Counselors do not work one party miracles in marriage very often. It takes two people working on the problem. The battle is already lost if only one person assumes responsibility. Many couples start counseling together with good intentions only to have one of them quit after a couple of sessions or take a dislike to the counselor at being probed and questioned. Too many expect a session or two to solve what fifteen years might have created. If one person refuses help, your chances are minimal that you will get your marriage back together.

3. *Has A Third Party Become Involved With Either Mate?*
   The breakup of a marriage may be caused by internal strife within the marriage or by a third party relationship being formed outside of the marriage. Since we do not have time to argue cause and effect here, we simply submit from experience that a third party involvement usually brings the marriage to its end. Some partners will wait, forgive, endure and try to forget. But the law of averages is pretty high that the third party involvement will end the marriage.

4. *What Have I Learned From My Past Experiences That Will Shed Light On My Present Situation?*
   Experience is, for all of us, a good teacher. We learn by living and by experiencing. We can all look into our well of experience and draw from it. Hopefully, you will not have to marry many times in order to learn from experience. Many marriages contain elements that were out of control long before the marriage was a reality. But many people would rather face hope than reality and they gamble that things will be different this time. Learn from your past!

Few people make dramatic changes in their life and life-style without some kind of outside help, whether God or professional. Just hoping a marriage will come back together by itself is like wishing on a chicken bone. Each person must evaluate for themselves whether the relationship has died or whether there is enough life to hold out some hope.

ADJUSTMENT—STAGE TWO

As the shock stage of a divorce begins to wear away, a process of adjustment—stage two—begins to take place. Adjustment means you begin to deal with the reality that this has really happened to you. Shock is accepting the facts of divorce, adjustment is doing something about it.

There is a period of time in most divorces that is similar to that experienced at the loss of a mate through death. It is a time of grief, mourning, or sorrow over a relationship that is lost. Just as people accept shock in different ways, people also accept mourning in different ways. They can go inward or outward.

POSITIVE MOURNING

Positive mourning is the experience of remembering the good, happy, fun-filled memories of your marriage and forgetting the bad memories. It's being glad you had the good times and wishing you still had them. It's being sorry that they are gone now and knowing that there is still much happiness left for you in life. Happiness is not born in marriage and killed in divorce. Positive mourning says I have the human right to feel loss, grief, sorrow. It says I hurt and for now there is an empty space in my life. I can cry because they are positive tears.

NEGATIVE MOURNING

Negative mourning is the experience of swimming in a sea of self-pity. It usually starts with the assumption that the marriage dissolution was all my fault or all his or her fault. Once this idea is projected, the person locks himself into a mental room and throws the key away. He defies others to break down the door and release him from his self-imposed misery. Life has dealt him a bad hand and his relief comes from telling everyone his miseries. Feeling sorry for yourself should be limited to a five second experience about once a week. It is self-defeating and often leads into deep mental depression. If you obtained all the pity that you wanted from others, what would you have? A warehouse full of "I'm so sorrys"!

ASSEMBLING THE PIECES

Jigsaw puzzle fans go about their hobby in an interesting way. They dump all the pieces of the puzzle on a table, turn them all right side up, then slowly begin putting them together.

Sometimes they leave the puzzle for a time and return to work on it later. The project methodically goes on until the last piece is in place. The picture is completed—success is attained.

Life is a daily process of putting the pieces of a puzzle together. We do a little each day and slowly the picture takes shape. In a divorce, the pieces to the puzzle get tossed all over the house and some are even lost for a while. Some get in the wrong place and don't fit too well. Persistence, perseverance and patience help us keep working on the puzzle. Slowly the pieces come together. In the adjustment stage, pieces to the puzzle are being identified, turned right side up and slowly put into place. Each chapter in this book will help you put some of the pieces of the divorce puzzle together. Adjustment sometimes means we can't have things exactly as we want them. We adjust to the situation as it is, knowing that it will change.

Adjustment is also a time of transition. It is passing from one life-style (married) to another life-style (single). Patterns of living that were firmly established in marriage have now been disrupted and the new pattern has not yet been fully developed. Adjustment is often marked by restlessness, disorganization and extreme highs and lows in feelings. Loneliness creeps in and out. And the burden of being a single parent can settle like an unyielding yoke upon your shoulders.

Adjustment sometimes means that you have to make very important decisions for yourself, family and future while you are at your emotional worst. The temptation is often to throw all the pieces of your puzzle into the air and hope that they will fall together when they land.

Take the time to sort the pieces out, place them right side up, and see if they fit together. Getting away from the puzzle for a while often helps you get the pieces into better perspective when you return.

The period of adjustment may take many months. Time is a healer and cannot be hurried. Many people in post divorce adjustment want to hurry the hurts away and experience instant new health. Divorce recovery takes time.

GROWTH—STAGE THREE

When was the last time you checked to see if the grass outside your house was still growing? That's silly. No one checks their grass. You just wait a week, it grows, you cut it, wait another week and it's time to cut it again. The point is that your grass grows even though you can't see it growing. Growth in human lives works the same way. You grow a little each day even if you can't see it or feel it. Good growth happens when conditions are right, both in lawns and in lives. Good growth begins when a person says, "I want to grow and learn from my experiences."

In a recent conversation, I asked a person how they were doing. The response was "not too good," followed by, "I'm going through a divorce."

The response was typical of most people. We are all going through different things each day. The difference is that you have a choice whether you will simply GO through it or GROW through it.

Growing through a divorce says I will learn all I can learn from this experience and I will be a stronger and better person because of this learning experience.

If anyone had come to you prior to your divorce and asked what you knew about divorce, you probably would have replied, "not very much." You possibly could have added that you had known people who had divorced, but you had little personal experience with the problem until now.

Growing is learning all you can about a given situation or thing. Divorce can be either a negative, self-defeating experience in your life or a positive growth producing experience. It depends on what you are willing to learn from it and how you put what you have learned into practice.

Let me share eight GROWING THROUGH DIVORCE steps with you.

1. Realize that time is a healer and you must walk through that process one day at a time. No one can walk through it for you. No one else will have your exact feelings and experiences. Some days the growth time will be an hour or maybe even half of a day. But you will only grow as you walk through the process.

2. Come to grips with yourself. You can't deny your existence no matter how frustrated, lonely, guilty, angry or desperate you may feel.

3. Set aside time for reflection, meditation, reading, thinking and personal growth. There are many situations around you that you will be powerless to change. But you can

always work on changing yourself. Allow yourself some time to do this.

4.   Get with healthy people who are struggling but growing. There is only minimal comfort in hearing other peoples' divorce stories while you are going through yours. At first it may be a help but it soon becomes a bore. Healthy people are those who let the past die and who live and grow in the present.

5.   Seek professional counseling or therapy if you feel you need it. Asking for help is a sign of strength, not weakness. Many counseling centers offer divorce recovery workshops that can be invaluable in helping you gain insight into your situation.

6.   Accept the fact that you are divorced (or divorcing) and now single. Many divorced people still feel married. A lady summed up her feelings one day by saying that she was not single but merely between marriages. If you are divorced, you are single.

7.   Put the past in the past and live in the present.

8.   Commit your new way to God, begin new things and seek the help and relationships you need to BEGIN AGAIN.

None of the above growth producing steps are easy. You have to begin where you are even if you feel you are fresh out of new beginnings.

Society has a way of looking at Divorce and spelling it F-A-I-L-U-R-E. Even though it is widely accepted as a way of life in our world, it still carries its brand on peoples lives. We somehow will give people the right to fail in business, in school, in careers, but not in marriage. The contemporary church, in particular, has looked upon divorce as the unforgivable sin while preaching that man is not perfect, must live with his humanity and has the freedom to fail. A divorced person has enough of a struggle living with his own weight of judgment without having that weight added to by others. Someone asked me recently who suffered the most in a divorce, a man, a woman or the children. My response was people!

GROWING
THROUGH
DIVORCE

2

LETTING GO

"I can only live in the present if I let go of the past."

One of the earliest hurdles to be faced in a divorce is the struggle of letting go of the many things that were a part of the marriage experience. Divorce brings a vast number of changes into the lives of those involved. One person described it recently as "the catapult from a four bedroom house in suburbia to an apartment in exile." Few people can go through a divorce with their old life and life-style remaining intact.

There are a few adventuresome persons who welcome changes

in life but most of us are somewhat threatened by changes and the fear of the unknown. Divorce forces people to change. Change involves letting go of old things and accepting new things.

Every life is maintained by various support systems. We grow and depend upon mental, physical, social and spiritual structures for our support. When any of these structures is weakened, we become confused, disoriented, frustrated, insecure, or uncertain. Divorce introduces numerous changes in each of these four areas.

MENTAL

The mental area is how we utilize our mind and how our mind reacts to what is going on around us. We develop attitudes in our mind towards our ex-spouse, our children, our relatives and our friends.

The state of marriage in these four supporting groups of people gives us one set of attitudes. The state of divorce usually reverses our attitudes to these people as well as their attitudes to us. Ex-spouse attitudes can go from love to hate overnight. The attitudes of children can vary from the divorce is all your fault to the divorce is all my fault. Relatives can line up on either spouse's team. Friends can choose their objectivity and choose sides or disappear completely.

Coping on the mental level with our own feelings and attitudes and with the feelings and attitudes of others can become an awesome burden. Learning to "let go" in this area means coming to the realization and recognition that I am responsible for my attitudes and feelings but not for the attitudes and feelings of others. There will be changes in other peoples' response to me that I can do very little about. Things will not remain as they were prior to the divorce. People will not remain as they were even though you wish they would. Divorce sets in motion the wheels of change in attitudes and relationships. Accepting and understanding this will help you live in the present rather than the past. First attitudes and reactions to a divorce are often not permanent ones. But divorce does affect other people around you and they have a right to their own response and attitudes.

SOCIAL

The social world of a person involves job-career, school-education, church-religion, community interaction, life-style. As a human being, we have a need to interact with other human beings. We form ties and relationships as we weave the fabric of our life-style about us. A divorce not only draws attitudes and reactions from those in our personal world, it calls for a response from those in our various social worlds.

Society is generally constructed for couples, pairs, twos. The ultimate of that coupling is marriage. When people divorce, the social world responds by asking how this will affect them more than how this will affect the people divorcing. The "what people think" syndrome takes over and judgements are made and verdicts are rendered. The social world often lets go of the divorcing person before the divorcing person has the chance to adjust or change their social involvements. A job can be lost and a career ended. School life and peer-teacher misunderstanding can be devastating to children. Attitudes of the church and organized religious life will be examined under the spiritual area. Involvements with various community agencies, clubs and organizations are often terminated. "I was married—I now am single," prompts a sudden shift in life-style from married friends to single friends. This often occurs after building only married friendships for twenty or more years.

Letting go in the social realm means I will have to face some changes, discriminations and reactions in this area. I cannot continue as before. But I will struggle and fight to maintain the involvements I want and I will work hard at building new and rewarding social involvements.

PHYSICAL

"One of the worst things about a divorce is coming home at the end of a day to an apartment or house and not having the physical presence of another adult to share your joys and sorrows with." This response is typical of the many I hear from formerly married persons who face the loss of a mate. Divorce brings about the loss of love but it also brings the removal of the physical presence of the other partner from the home. Not having someone there to talk things over with—no one to laugh with and to cry with—can be the most awesome burden to the divorced person. Loneliness creates a hostile environment in which fears are heightened. All divorced persons must face the reality that they stand as one, not two. Many people stay in a marriage long after the love has gone just so they will not physically be alone.

Letting go in the physical area means slowly accepting the reality that the other person is not there any longer and will never be there again. Accepting this reality means accepting the hurt of being alone. But being alone right now is not a life sentence imposed as a penalty for your divorce.

The physical area may also involve the loss of a home environment. Someone has said that a house is where you live, a home is what people make that house into. I resent the use of the term "a broken home" to describe a divorce. A broken home seems to convey to me the idea that it is permanently destroyed and the people who have lived there are beyond repair. If you allow a divorce to give you a "broken home," it will. A better attitude and response would be to acknowledge that your home environment was dented, dinged, bent or bruised. These terms admit damage but do not preclude repair.

In the world of automobile accidents, "totalled" means your car is not worth fixing. A divorce may make you feel "totalled" and beyond repair in all areas. But don't believe it! Your life may not be the shiny new model it was at the marriage altar but the dents and scratches that a divorce has made in it can be repaired with your help, the help of others and the help of God.

SPIRITUAL

A divorce can drive you away from God or drive you to God. In my personal counseling, many people tell me that their divorce has caused them to re-examine their relationship to God. They have realigned their priorities and commitments to God and the church. The church, however, does not always make it easy on the divorced person to affirm faith and experience forgiveness.

Many people who experience divorce while involved in church and religious life are asked to move their membership and families elsewhere. Others are removed from future leadership roles in the life of the church and are imprisoned in the pews as a permanent penance for their misdeeds.

Spiritual isolation is often experienced by the religious person who goes through a divorce while the non-religious is attracted to the church that seeks to understand, have empathy and shows forgiveness. There are too few churches however that welcome the formerly married.

Letting go in the spiritual area means giving your divorce situation over to God and letting Him weigh it, judge it and balance it. It means knowing the difference between God's forgiveness and other people's lack of forgiveness. It means understanding that God is the author of new beginnings.

A NEW IDENTITY

Letting go of old things means replacing them with new things. New things have to be acknowledged and accepted on the mental level before they can be lived out on the physical, social and spiritual levels.

Many divorced persons tell me that they feel married, act married but live single. Growth in divorce is accepting its realities. In a divorce workshop that I teach, we ask people to repeat out loud the following sentences:

"I AM DIVORCED. I AM SINGLE. I AM O.K."

At first, it is mumbled rather softly. After a couple of times, it is said more firmly. Why do we do this? Because many people feel one way but have to live another. We try to help them get reality, feelings and living together. It starts by making a positive mental statement of who you are. When a person loses their identity, they are not sure who they are. In order to be healthy and growing, they must have an identity again. And they must accept what they are whether they like it or not.

KEYS TO ACCEPTING A NEW IDENTITY

1. Don't keep living in the role of the old identity. The longer you do this, the longer you will block the potential for new growth. You are not married so don't play the role. You are single and you must slowly discover what this new role is like and how to enact it.

2. Create "new experiences in living" for yourself. It's easy to live and relive your old experiences. Creating new experiences in living will help you become an adventurer in the present rather than a tenant of the past.

3. Don't let other people superimpose an identity upon you. It's sometimes easier to become what other people want us to be rather than what we really want to be. Form your own identity. You are YOU, not what someone else is or thinks you are.

4. Learn all you can about your new identity and how to live it. Being single, being a single parent, being a weekend parent, being alone, being resourceful, being independent, being a new person.

5. Realize that you are a unique, unrepeatable, miracle of God. Developing a relationship with God gives foundation to your new identity.

6. Know that you have the freedom to fail. We live with our humanity and that humanity causes us to make mistakes. Take risks and learn from your failures.

HOW LONG DOES IT TAKE?

We all live by the clock. We alternately try to save time and waste time. Many divorced persons want to know how long it will take to get over their divorce and the many hurts experienced in it. How long will it be before I feel good, whole, and together again? How long does it take to fall in love? How long does it take to fall out of love?

It all takes time! For some a short amount, for others a long time. Some heal quickly and forget easily. Others heal slowly and never forget. Decide for yourself right now that you will *take* all the time you need to let go of old things and build new things—that you will not become impatient but will understand that this is a new and growing experience for you.

PERSONAL GROWTH AND DISCUSSION QUESTIONS

1. How did the following supportive people react to your divorce? Ex-spouse, children, relatives, friends.

2. What effect has your divorce had upon the social areas of your life?

3. How do you handle the absence of a 'physical presence' in your home?

4. What effect did your divorce have in the spiritual areas of your life?

5. What plan do you have for developing a new identity for yourself?

6. My personal goal for this week is

_____

_____

_____

_____

_____

GROWING
THROUGH
DIVORCE

3

GETTING THE
EX-SPOUSE IN FOCUS

"I loved you, I hate you, I'll get you."

"How can the feelings for an ex-spouse go so rapidly from love to hate to revenge?"

I've been asked that question many times by many people who are caught at the feeling level in their divorce. Conditions and situations can cause the feelings in a person to go from one extreme to another in the short space of seconds or the lengthened span of years.

Divorce, unlike death, does not fully remove the ex-spouse from daily existence. Ex-spouses hover about the edges of a marriage dissolution and frequently wreck havoc with the other mates life. Different reactions of the involved parties in a divorce often relate directly to the causes that led to the divorce.

There are seven basic causes of divorce that seem to appear with the most frequency.

1. The "Victim" Divorce

    The victim divorce is a setting where one mate leaves the home for another person. It may be a secretary, close friend, old friend, new friend, etc. The results are the same. One person wants the divorce while the other person does not. The mate left behind may suffer feelings of rejection, guilt, worthlessness and despair that can soon turn into anger and revenge. Hostility toward the ex-spouse is usually the highest in the victim divorce.

2. The "Problem" Divorce

    The reason for this kind of divorce is because of a "prolem" the other mate had. Common problems are alcohol, gambling, money, or sex. Some people bring their prolems into the marriage with them while other problems are created within and because of the marriage. Spousal feelings in this kind of divorce runs from sympathy for the ex-mate to the regret that so many years were given to this kind of existence. The person with the problem may feel anger and hostility at being "abandoned."

3. The "Little Boy, Little Girl" Divorce

    This divorce is prompted by the fact that one mate or the other decides that they don't want the responsibility of being husband or wife, or mother or father. They decide that they want to spend their time with the "boys" or the "girls" and play with the kind of toys they played with before marriage. The only difference is the price of the toys. Personal immaturity and the lack of learning to assume responsibility brings on the divorce. Feelings here are centered in rejection.

4. The "I Was Conned" Divorce
   In simplest terms, this means that one mate or the other did not get what they thought they were getting in the marriage. The inability of one person to be honest with the other often leads to disillusionment and divorce later. This kind of divorce usually leads to a defensiveness toward the ex-spouse and a general distrust of the opposite sex.

5. The "Shotgun" Divorce
   Most people have heard of the "shotgun" wedding. It is usually intitiated by the fact that the bride-to-be is pregnant and family, friends and community feel the honorable way to resolve the problem is by marriage. In many instances, shotgun weddings bring about shotgun divorces. Shotgun marriages involve living under the gun for both parties and marriage by coercion doesn't always work too well. Feelings for the ex-spouse in this divorce setting run from pity to rejection.

6. The "Menopause" Divorce
   We know that women go through menopause but there is a growing belief in some medical circles that men go through some kind of state similar to menopause in women. In both sexes, dramatic changes in personality and behavior can cause one mate or the other to leave the marriage. Attitudes toward the ex-spouse after this kind of divorce are centered in lack of understanding and a general confusion as to what really happened. Because this can happen after many years of marriage, a deep hurt and bitterness is coupled to an abandoned feeling.

7. The "No Fault" Divorce
   A few years ago, divorcing parties had to state the causes for the divorce. Charges and counter charges were filed. Witnesses were brought forth to testify to the truth or lack of it. With the changing divorce laws in many states, there is no cause or reason needed. No one is held at fault. Often, two people just decide that they have had it with each other. They want to go their separate ways. Feelings in this kind of divorce are usually very neutral. They feel it just didn't work out and it wasn't anyones fault.

Getting along with an ex-spouse when feelings and hurt levels are running high demands a great deal of patience and understanding. If no children are involved in the divorce or if the children are grown, married and out of the home, there is only minimal need for ongoing personal contact or confrontation. Where children are involved, the reminders of the heartaches and hurts are highly visible. In the immediate post divorce days, the conflict level between spouses is generally highest. As time passes and new interests and relationships are formed, the conflict level subsides. Visitations, support payments, vacations, daily problems seem to fall into an acceptable pattern of existence. The hurts remain but the aggravation level seems to go down. Growth in dealing with an ex-spouse takes place when your feelings of hostility, hatred and revenge mellow first to feelings of guilt and being sorry for yourself and your ex-spouse and finally to feelings of indifference and acceptance. This process of time and working through your feelings may take several years. There is no instant cure although many search for it. Feelings are healed in time. Growth in new areas will modify your feelings.

People who experience divorce will often find that their

feelings for the ex-mate will vary from day to day. When they don't see the person, they may find themselves wanting a reunion. When they do see the person, they may experience disgust, hatred and hurt. It is easy to live in the dream world of what a person was rather than what a person is. Sometimes the inability to start a new life will send a person back to the old mate. Fear of the new in this instance can become greater than the fear of the old.

Here are several growth guidelines in getting the ex-spouse in focus:

1. *Take the detachment a day at a time.* One of the soundest principles I know in working your way through a divorce is to simply take things a day at a time. Wishing tomorrow were here will not make today go away. Worrying about the future will not help you live in the present. Decide to live each day as it comes. Emotional healing can be slower than any physical healing you have ever experienced. Get used to living in the "NOW." Problems are resolved one day at a time. Plans are made one day at a time. Most people experiencing divorce feel that they are just not going to make it. They feel this way because they spend most of their mental energies racing backward into the past or forward into the future.

   When the future is uncertain, there is a great tendency to simply worry about it. Worry never changes anything. The Apostle Paul shared some wise words on worry with an early group of Christians. He said, "Be anxious for nothing, but in everything by prayer and supplication with thanksgiving, let your requests be made known to God. And the peace of God, which surpasses all comprehension, shall guard your

hearts and your minds in Christ Jesus.'' (Philippians 4:
6, 7). You only need strength for today. As you test your
strength on each day, you will build a reservoir for all your
tomorrows.

Losing a person from your life that was once so important
and intergral to your existence is extremely hard. In many
marriages, peoples identities are so closely interwoven that
they feel they cease to exist without the other person. You
do exist. You are alive. You will make it through today!

2. *Try to make the break as clean as possible.* Many divorced
persons don't know how to "quit their marriage." They
keep struggling to free themselves from the ex-spouse while
secretly wanting to hold on. Some ex-mates use every
opportunity to see the other person and then regret it after
having done so. They might keep hoping that the other
person has changed or that their memory of the bad things
will go away. Many departed mates return at will to their
former home for meals, evenings, baby-sitting, gardening,
repairs or nostalgia. Sometimes at "visiting-dinner guest"
level, former mates find themselves quite compatible and
friendly. Remember that visiting together is vastly different from living together. Three months of separation is
seldom able to heal twenty years of hurts and problems.

In most instances, physical separation should initiate a
clean break between ex-mates. A lingering post divorce
attachment will prohibit the establishing of a new identity
and positive growth.

Visitation rights where children are involved should be
established and followed. Maintenance of the home should
be planned and adhered to. The paying of support

payments should not be used as an admission ticket to the former home.

Seeing an ex-mate usually does very little for the personal ego. It only reminds one of the past and the things they no longer have. It doesn't change anything. The sooner you begin building a new life for yourself, the happier you will be.

I have known people who decide to divorce and still live in the same house for extended periods of time. I have known others who separate but still maintain a dating relationship. These and other continuing relationships after a divorce has been decided upon, will only prohibit you from experiencing a new beginning and a new sense of personal self-worth.

3. *Quit accepting responsibility for the ex-spouse.* Many of us feel responsible in life for things that we can't control. A vital part of mature growth is learning to accept responsibility for yourself as we state in Chapter Four. A further part of that maturity is to let others accept responsibility for themselves. Many ex-mates feel an ongoing responsibility for their ex-partner. They may wonder if the ex can make it alone, if they will commit suicide, if they will go hungry, if they will have a nervous breakdown. All of these concerns and many others may be felt for the ex-mate. Attempts to mother or father an ex-spouse often follow hard on the heels of an emotion-wrenching divorce.

Few people learn to stand alone and discover their own resources until they have to. Children will let their parents do all the work and worry for as long as they can. Some divorcing people revert back to a child dependence state.

Sometimes it is an attempt to have their personal needs met, and sometimes it is an attempt to make the other person feel guilty.

Don't get caught in the trap of assuming responsibility for the ex-spouse, other than what the law stipulates. Don't spend all your time wondering if the ex-spouse is going to make it. They will and can make it if they choose to. If they decide to infect themselves with an eternal case of the "WOE ME'S," they will only prohibit their own growth. Don't let them prohibit yours by hooking you into being responsible for them.

4. *Don't let your children intimidate you.* The secret desire of many children is that their parents will get back together again. And that is a natural and acceptable feeling. Children often don't understand the private lives and private wars that adults have. They only know that they want their parents together again.

A child that continually talks about this can inflict on a parent a foreboding burden of guilt. The end result can be a frustrating attempt to fan to life the fires of a long dead marriage in order to please the child. Remember you are an adult and children do not always understand adult decisions.

Children have their own ways of getting at a parent. The desired outcome of their intentions might be very honorable but at a deep level, they are probably more concerned that their needs are met than yours.

There are hundreds of games that a child can play to intimidate a parent. They often begin with statements like: "All my friends have a mother and father who live with them." "Why did *you* make daddy (or mommy) move away?" "Is it my fault that daddy (or mommy) doesn't live here anymore?"

These heartrending comments from a child can cause many a parent to race back to a former mate for another try or to fervently pursue a new replacement for the departed parent.

Love and try to understand your children but don't let them intimidate you.

5. *Don't get trapped in your "child" state.* First Corinthians, Chapter Thirteen in the Bible is known as the Love Chapter. Verse eleven simply states: "When I was a child, I used to speak as a child, think as a child, reason as a child; when I became a man, I did away with childish things."

It is easy to get trapped into childish behavior with an ex-spouse. Childish behavior with an "ex" may involve temper tantrums, getting even, telling lies, jealousy, fighting, etc. These things can happen when we forget who we are. A child can go from liking a friend to "hating" a friend in the short space of an hours play. Many adults apparently have the same capacity.

I love you, I hate you, I'll get you, seems to adequately describe many post divorce relationships. Vast amounts of mental and physical energies are spent in childish hate campaigns. Arriving five minutes late for visitation or debating about who gets the color television and who gets the black and white, can cause once loving couples to become violently warring ones.

Divorce seems a ready catapult that launches people back into their childish behavior patterns. Considerateness, kindness and honesty are relegated to another place in time. How tragic and demeaning to ones personhood.

Growth in divorce is treating an ex-spouse as an adult. It is not seeking reprisal and vindication even if you feel deserving of it. Negative and childish treatment of an ex-mate is immature and a constant drain on your emotional level. Warring people are in a constant state of battle tension. Little positive growth is attained until the fight is declared over.

Becoming an adult means childish speaking, thinking and reasoning are abandoned.

In the heat of conflict, argument and despair, we often forget who we are. Divorce is often described as a war with all the tactics and strategy of war put to use. If that is the case, I would plead that the warriors in divorce come to a quick and lasting truce. Nothing is gained by broken and hostile relationships.

If a divorce has to happen, let it become history as quickly as possible and let the relationships of ex-mates take on a mature form of behavior and existence. Everyone benefits when people are treated with respect and dignity. In your dealings with your ex-spouse, tell them that your part of the war is over! If they continue to fight, let it be their problem and don't continue to supply them with ammunition.

PERSONAL GROWTH AND DISCUSSION QUESTIONS

1. Which one of the seven basic causes of divorce describes your divorce?

2. Describe your current feelings towards your ex-spouse.

3. How would you like to feel about your ex-spouse?

4. Which one of the growth guidelines in getting the ex-spouse in focus is the most difficult for you? The easiest?

5. Are you currently treating your ex-spouse as a child or an adult?

6. My personal goal for this next week is

_____

_____

_____

_____

_____

GROWING
THROUGH
DIVORCE

4

ASSUMING RESPONSIBILITIES
FOR MYSELF

"Will somebody out there please make me happy?"

Who is responsible for you and your happiness? Your ex-spouse? Your children? Your boss? Your family? Your friends? God?

Many people would like to give someone else the responsibility for making them happy. It is easy to blame your unhappiness on other people. But reality says that you are responsible for YOURSELF and that it's no one else's job to make you happy.

People often marry other people with the assumption that the person they are marrying will make them happy. What an awesome responsibility is placed upon that person's shoulders. What if they fail? Who gets the blame? Where can other happiness be found? A marriage built upon that premise often leads to a divorce and unless the lesson is learned, the hunt is on for another person to provide happiness.

Many divorced persons feel that the answer to all their problems will be found in finding the right person. I call this the "abdication of responsibility syndrome." It often leads to a quick second, third, fourth, etc. marriage.

Divorce can be a teacher if you will let it. It will teach you how, as an adult, you can assume responsibility for yourself, your thoughts and your actions. Persons who GROW through divorce experience this. They can go from a marriage that was a total dependency into a divorce that teaches personal responsibility.

A child learns very young that he is spared punishment and responsibility if he can blame his actions or deeds on someone else. We begin to build a pattern in youth that affects our later years. It is easy to come to the place where we always blame someone else for our situation, misdeeds, problems, struggles, lack of growth, or misfortunes. I listen to many people say "If only I would have . . . we would not be divorced today." Assuming responsibility for yourself may be a new discovery for you. It begins in the following areas.

1. I ASSUME RESPONSIBILITY FOR MY PART OF THE FAILURE OF MY MARRIAGE. One of the insidious traps that divorced persons get caught in, is playing the blame game. One or more can play the game but no one ever wins.

Every action in a marriage draws a reaction. Actions and reactions build for years, one person explodes and leaves and the blame game starts. No one can relive the years of a marriage and change what is history. But accepting responsibility for *your* part of the failure can certainly change your future. PEOPLE DON'T DIVORCE SITUATIONS, THEY DIVORCE PEOPLE WHO CREATE SITUATIONS AND FAIL TO TAKE RESPONSIBILITY FOR THOSE SITUATIONS.

In a divorce, assuming responsibility for yourself does not start with your future, it starts with your past and putting that in perspective. It means expressing *your* responsibility for the failures in your marriage to your ex-spouse. If both parties do this, the blame game will come to an end and postmarital relationships will not be warring ones.

2. I ASSUME RESPONSIBILITY FOR MY PRESENT SITUATION. I frequently hear people blame their present situation, whether it is housing, lack of money, job, etc. on their past. It is easy to say everything is bad because of what I have just gone through. This kind of situation is known as the "Woe Me's." Many get caught in the routine of wishing things were different. They are hooked on extracting pity from others that will reinforce for them the fact that they are merely the victim of circumstances and powerless to handle or change their present situation.

If you do not assume responsibility for your present situation, who will? Part of being an adult is accepting responsibility. If you are a single parent with children at home, a house to maintain, money to earn, a job to pursue, you will not get the job done by endless television watching, bar hopping, chain smoking and retreating from life because it has given you a raw deal. Being responsible says you need to assess your present situation and the needs you have. Make a list with the heading at the top reading I AM RESPONSIBLE FOR: Be honest and don't pass the buck. Then draw a line down the center of the page. At the head of the second column write I WILL FULFILL THIS RES-PONSIBILITY BY: Spend some time on this. Share it with a friend for further input. In effect you are accepting and articulating your responsibilities for right now and setting goals to achieve their fulfillment. Things that are frightening in our mind usually become obtainable realities when placed on paper.

3. I ASSUME RESPONSIBILITY FOR MY FUTURE. There are many people who live their entire lives with contingency goals. These are not real goals but negative goals that are based upon circumstances and other people. They change constantly as people come and go in our lives. Examples are:

> I won't go to work because I might remarry.
> I won't go back to school because I might fail.
> I won't date because I might get hurt again.
> I won't move because I might not get as good a situation as I have.
> I'll do this until something better comes along.
> I won't set goals because they might interfere with someone I'll meet.

I could add numerous other statements I hear people make every day. Instead of securing their own future with constructive plans and growth producing goals, they make no moves for fear they will make the wrong ones.

Many people are divorcing today after twenty and thirty years of marriage. When I ask these people what goals they have set for themselves, they often respond by saying its too late or that their goal is just to survive each day. Someone has said, "Shoot at nothing and that is what you will hit."

No one else is responsible for your future but you. You have to live in it. Accept responsibility for it. Make the best plans for you. Whether you remain single or remarry should not affect your present planning. You do not have to be married to be headed somewhere in life.

4. I ASSUME RESPONSIBILITY FOR MYSELF. During college, we often discussed whether environment or heredity played the biggest part in our personality development. The arguments were good but no one ever seemed to prove one or the other. A fitting conclusion would be that both play a great deal in who we are today. If we are successful today, we can attribute it to our successful influences. Determining causes does not change present realities. Each of us is responsible for ourselves. We cannot renege that responsibility. Three basic areas in self-responsibility are: thoughts, feelings and actions.

THOUGHTS
What does a divorced person think about?
Why has this happened to me?
What went wrong?
What will I do now?
Can I make it on my own?
How long will I hurt?
Can I ever be happy again?

These and countless hundreds of other thoughts race through your mind every day. Many of these thoughts are negative, self defeating and guilt producing. When negative thoughts build up in the mind, they lead to negative feelings and actions. A divorced person who spends too much time in the negative world runs the risk of becoming lonely, bitter and depressed. If you spend too much time thinking about all the things that led to your divorce and all the present dangers it has created, your mind will not be free to be constructive and clear in dealing with the realities of today.

Closing the door on the past means closing out the dead thoughts and replacing them with positive thoughts of the present and future. You can control what you think about. For many divorced persons, the lonely hours just prior to or after bedtime trigger the mind into the thoughts of yesterday or worrying about tomorrow.

You can control what you think about! Don't waste mental energy on things you cannot change and have no control over. You are responsible for your thoughts.

FEELINGS

"How are you feeling?" *Fine. Terrible. Tired. Happy. Sad. Depressed. Lonely. Hot. Cold.*

Feelings are! I do not choose whether or not to have feelings. They come out of nowhere, sometimes when I am least expecting them. In themselves, feelings are neither good nor bad. I am responsible for what I do with my feelings but I am not responsible for having them. Everyone has feelings.

But not everyone is in touch with the feelings they have. Being in touch with my feelings means I can identify my feelings and deal with them in a conscious and constructive manner.

52

Divorced persons have feelings. They have feelings whether they have been wronged or are in the wrong. They have a right to express their feelings.

One of the finest ways to communicate with another person in an area that may raise a conflict is to preface what you are saying with, "My feeling about that is . . ." Most people come from the judgment side and issue pronouncements rather than simply sharing their feelings.

Here are three things to remember in getting your feelings expressed:

1. Get in touch with the feelings inside you.
2. Develop the freedom to express those feelings.
3. Learn to live comfortably with your feelings.

Feelings need to be identified and expressed. Repressed feelings cause depression, guilt and hostility towards others. Learn to share your feelings.

ACTIONS

"Stop it! Don't act like that!"
"I can't help it. You made me do it!"

How many times as a child did someone reprimand you for your actions? And you tried to place the blame for your actions on someone else. We expect children to react like that but somehow, when we grow up, we expect adult behavior. And adult behavior teaches that we assume responsibility for our actions and we stop blaming them on other people.

An important key to growth in divorce is assuming responsibility for your actions. Blaming your present actions on another person's treatment of you does not release you from responsibility. Taking charge of yourself means you act on situations rather than react to situations. Check on yourself for a few days and see how many times you are caught reacting rather than acting. Reacting puts the results in someone else's ball park. Acting keeps them in your ball park and leaves you in control of the situation. Ex-mates often spend a great deal of time reacting to each other. Feelings and emotions become so overloaded that there is great explosive reaction and very little chance for positive action. Reactions trigger defense mechanisms that cause a person to either fight or retreat. Acting on a situation means I hear what is being said, I think about what is being said and I respond to what is being said. I present a clear statement of my feelings that will lead to my positive actions.

Assuming responsibility for yourself is not an easy process. Like everything else, it takes time. There is no other honest way to face the reality of your divorce. You have to build a new identity and in order to do that, you have to take charge of yourself. After many years of dependent living, that may be extremely difficult. Divorce will either force you to assume responsibility by saying, "I can" or send you looking for someone else to do it for you.

PERSONAL GROWTH AND DISCUSSION QUESTIONS

1. What are some of the areas in your marriage where you feel you failed?

2. What are some of the struggles you are having in assuming responsibility for your present situation?

3. Are your goals set by you or are they "contingency goals" that are dependent upon other people and situations?

4. In what area do you have the greatest struggle: Thoughts, Feelings, Actions? Explain.

5. My personal goal for this next week is

_____

_____

_____

_____

_____

_____

GROWING
THROUGH
DIVORCE

5

ASSUMING RESPONSIBILITIES
FOR MY CHILDREN

*"Divorce is the process
that turns whole parents into half parents."*

Single parenthood usually starts at the moment the children are told that mommy and daddy no longer love each other or want to continue living in the same house. The announcement to the children of the impending divorce can either cause them to echo a sigh of relief, or a sob of terror. Inwardly or outwardly, children think about or ask about what will happen to them. Where will they live? With whom will they live? How will things change? Will they ever see the departing parent again? As someone has said, "If divorce can be likened to war, then children are its orphans."

Assuming the responsibility of being a single parent is awesome, frightening, challenging and rewarding. Few parents embarking upon the experience feel they can do well. But most learn to do it and do a very good job at it. The common fear is that if child raising was hard with two parents in the home, it will be impossible with only one parent. It takes a great deal of adjusting but it is not impossible. Assuming and continuing the responsibility of being a single parent is equally important whether you are a weekday mother or father or a weekend mother or father.

SINGLE PARENT PROBLEMS

"My Circuits are on Overload"

If marriages are strained and overtaxed with the problem of too little money, divorce is equally overloaded with too little money and too many problems. Single parents complain about too many decisions that have to be made without the consultation of another partner, too many jobs to be done by one person that were once divided by two, too many tensions and frustrations that seemingly have only intermediate solutions, and too little time apart from child rearing that you can claim as your own. For the parent with custody rights it's too much children too much of the time. For the parent without custody rights it's too little children too much of the time. One suffers overload and one suffers loneliness. And the hurt is equal on the emotional level.

58

Few divorcing partners find the balancing point on the "too much or too little" where the children are concerned. Too often the children become excess baggage to be packed and shuffled from station to station.

"Where Are You When I Need You?"

In many divorce situations, the weekend or visiting parent may become a parent by proxy or consultation only. He or she may only be called upon at a time of a crisis, discipline or decision. Often these needs concern the health of a child, medical or dental decisions, parent-teacher academic needs or personal behavioral problems of the child. Being a parent by proxy is not easy. Decisions have to be made based only on the facts given, which may or may not be accurate. An absentee parent often has to assume the role of judge.

The custody parent has the problem of contacting and invading the realm of the departed parent with a constant stream of problems. When there are no problems, there is no contact. Resentment can build on both sides. You are not there when I need you versus you only need me when you have a problem. The string of financing is often held by the non-custody parent and used as a weapon to achieve what he or she might want.

"I Don't Get Any Respect"

Divorcing parents can beat each other down verbally to the point where the children lose respect for them and sometimes for themselves. An "out of house parent" is seldom around to defend themselves from verbal abuse. The very act of leaving the home may force a child to lose respect for the parent. A child may think, "If they loved me, they would not leave." A constant barrage of "your mother did this or your father did that" is not very affirming in the growth of a child. With the loss of respect comes the problem of getting the children to mind. When respect goes, disobedience is soon to follow. Child discipline can quickly become a problem and more often than not, the children are left to roam and do as they please.

"Help, I'm A Prisoner"

Single parents can easily become a prisoner of their children. They may overcompensate in every area for the departed parent. They allow their children to restrict their mobility in their social and dating life. If they go out at all, they feel guilty at leaving the children alone or with a sitter. A single parent can allow this to be a serious barrier to their own growth and development.

A parent that confines themselves to their work and their children alone will become a prisoner in their own home. Your own emotional health and well being are important.

GUIDELINES FOR SUCCESSFUL SINGLE PARENTING

1. *Don't try to be both parents to your children.* Be what you are—a mother or a father. Many single parents make the deadly mistake of trying to fill both parent roles in the family. A single parent assumes some of the jobs the other parent did, but not the role of that parent. Trying to be a super parent will only bring you frustration and fatigue. Inform your children that you have no intention of filling the role of the departed parent but

that you are going to work very hard at being the best at what you are. I meet many single parents who are exhausted at trying to do everything and be everything so that their children will not be deprived at having only one parent in the home. Improve what you are and don't try to be what you are not.

2. *Don't force your children into playing the role of the departed parent.* This can start by telling a nine year old boy that he has to be the daddy of the house now or by telling a ten year old daughter that she is the mommy now. This places an incredible weight on a childs' shoulders. They are forced into playing a role that they neither understand nor are ready for. The desire of the parent is for them to fill in so that they won't have to face the reality of the situation. A child needs to be a child. They cannot fill an adults place so don't force them to. Let them be who they are. Again, they may have to assume some new jobs but not a new personality and identity.

3. *Be the parent you are.* Don't abdicate your parent position for that of a big brother, big sister, friend, buddy or pal. Some parents want a role change so that they won't have to assume the responsibility of being a single parent. Children have their friends and buddies. They deeply resent having their parent try to invade their world. Single parents who force their way into their children's world are only looking for a way of escape and not for the best interests of their children. Children need the security of the parent image, even more after one parent has left the home. They cannot afford to lose both parents. After divorce, they need to have a parent more firmly in his or her role than ever.

4. *Be honest with your children.* Tell them the truth about what is going on. The Bible tells us to speak the truth in love. I believe that means we tell the truth in a loving framework remembering that others are connected with our truth. Many single parents never really talk to their children about what has happened, how they feel about it and how the children feel about it. They may make promises that the other parent will return, that the other parent really loves them, etc., when reality does not bear this out and the parent becomes a liar to the child. Richard Gardner in his book, *The Boys and Girls Book About Divorce*, is a strong advocate of telling children the truth. He says, "Half-truths produce confusion and distrust, whereas truth, albeit painful, engenders trust and gives the child the security of knowing exactly where he stands. He is then in a better position to handle situations effectively."

5. *Don't put your ex-spouse down in front of your children.* In most divorces, the parents enter into the never ending game of trying to convince the children how bad the other parent is and how this divorce is all their fault. Each parent desperately wants the child to take their side in the conflict. It's a game that nobody wins and eventually causes the child to lose all respect for either parent. Most children don't really care who did what to whom. What they care about is what is going to happen to them. Let your children decide things for themselves. If you have to talk about your ex-spouse in front of your children, make it positive, not negative.

6. *Don't make your children undercover agents who report on the other parent's current activities.* Children resent having to spy on what a parent is doing. Often the reporting back is

done by subtle questioning and gentle prying. A good conversation upon the return of a child from being with the other parent would be:

"Hi! Did you have a nice time?"

"Yes, we did."

"Good. I'm glad."

A child has the right to privately enjoy a parent. What that person is saying, doing, buying, thinking, etc. is their business. Don't force your children into playing "I Spy."

7. *The children of divorce need both a mother and a father.* Don't deny them this right because of your anger, hostility, guilt or vengeance.

Some single parents feel that a departing parent has no rights to continue the relationship with the children. About the only way a court of law would agree with that would be if the parent might cause emotional or bodily harm to the child. Courts recognize the rights of both parents. The Judge of the Superior Court in Santa Ana, California gives divorcing parents a brochure entitled, "Parents Are Forever." Children need the right of access to both parents. Infrequently a parent will give up that right and not want to see the child. In most cases, though, parents feel very strongly about seeing their children. Let your children pursue that relationship as they desire. They will only have one natural mother and father. Don't let the acts or deeds or your feelings about the departed parent deny your child the right to a continuing relationship with that parent.

8. *Don't become a "Disneyland Daddy" or a "Magic Mountain Mommy."* California abounds with entertainment centers. On any weekend of the year, you will find crowds of

single parents fulfilling their visitation rights with their children. Tragically, the single parent outside of the home often becomes the entertainer. Not knowing what else to do with the children, taking, buying and doing seem to provide a way out of the guilt and absence from the home. As the supply of things to do and places to go becomes exhausted, weekend visits may become less frequent.

Children need to see the departed parent in a real life setting. Have them stay overnight at your home or apartment. Let them keep some of their belongings at your residence. If space allows, give them their own room. Let them cook, help with the chores and be a part of your world. Don't try to buy them. It will make them uncomfortable. It will also put you in the wrong role and be a hard act for the "at home" parent to follow.

9. *Share your dating life and social interests with your children.* After a parent departs the home, any adult that is introduced to the children by either parent is looked upon as a potential new mother or father. If the children are small, they might ask outright, "Are you my new mommy or daddy?" At times, this proves to be embarrassing to both parties. Older children may respond with an aloofness or outright hostility at a potential new parent. Children never ask the question, "How will this affect you?" They want to know how this person might affect them. They want to know how it will affect their relationship with the other parent as well. On the other hand, hiding your date and never informing the children what is going on will be a greater threat than keeping them informed about your feelings and talking to them openly about the developing relationship.

10. *Help your children keep the good memories of your past marriage alive.* Good memories are worth keeping. They help us become what we are. I recently heard of a single parent who burned all the family pictures that had the other mate in them. You have no right to rob your children of their happy memories. Keep the things that are important to them as well as to you. If they want to recall good things from the past and talk about them, let them. They have their memories too.

11. *Work out a management and existence structure for your children with your ex-spouse.* It is a tragedy of our times that the courts become the arbitrator of continuing relationships with children after divorce. Two adults should be able to sit down together and work out things that will lend to the best growth and development of the children. This may not happen in the emotional heat of the pre and post divorce setting. But when feelings cool and perspectives are regained, separated parents should be able to face the reality that child raising goes on and should go on as smoothly as possible for the welfare of the children. Divorce may claim you and your ex-spouse as its victims. Don't let it claim your children as well. An outside or third party source such as a divorce counselor can give valuable assistance in helping you set up a management structure for your children.

12. *If possible, try not to disrupt the many areas in your children's lives that offer them safety and security.* The same house, school, friends, church, and clubs will help maintain a balance that can offset to a degree the loss of a parent. Sometimes this is not possible and if a move is forthcoming, talk

it over with the children and let them have a part in the decision making. Present it as an adventure rather than a threat.

13. *If your child does not resume normal development and growth in his life within a year of the divorce, he may need the special care and help of a professional counselor.* During a divorce, a child can become a problem at school, grades can go down, interest in hobbies can vanish, a general attitude of restlessness and disobedience can set in. Some of this is normal. Children go through the stages of shock, adjustment and growth too. If negative patterns continue after a number of months, seek help. A few words by a trained professional can often turn the corner of post divorce adjustment for children.

Being a single parent is a skill to be learned. It is both lonely and rewarding. Many children grow up in one parent homes and have all the skills and attributes of children who grow up in two parent homes. Being a single parent does not assure your children of failure or success. A child can GROW THROUGH DIVORCE too.

PERSONAL GROWTH AND DISCUSSION QUESTIONS

1. How do your children relate to the absentee parent?

2. What is the biggest problem you face in being a single parent?

3. Evaluate your current relationship with your children.

4. How did you tell your children about your divorce? What was their reaction?

5. How honest have you been with your children about your divorce?

6. What kind of picture of your ex-spouse do you present to your children?

7. My personal goal for this next week is

_____

_____

_____

_____

_____

GROWING
THROUGH
DIVORCE

6

ASSUMING RESPONSIBILITY
FOR MY FUTURE

"Plan ahead . . . you have to live there!"

I ask many people who are experiencing divorce how they feel about their future. They often reply by saying, "What future?" The response is a natural one. The clouds of emotion, doubt, tension and the unknown tend to obliterate the thoughts of a clear and promising tomorrow. Planning ahead will seem very unrealistic when your mind is filled with the thoughts of yesterday and the current problems of today. Your future can be a threat or a promise depending upon your attitude and plans.

YES, YOU HAVE A FUTURE

Unless you die instantly while reading these lines, you will have a future. No one is certain of how long or how short it will be. Growth in divorce is assuming responsibility for your future, whether it is a long one or a short one. A divorced person sometimes has a greater will to die than to live. Death might seem honorable while life seems threatening. But positive planning for your future will give you the excitement of living in today. You have a future and it is entirely up to you to make plans to live in it. It is your responsibility and no one can do it for you. A wise person once said that there are three things that make for happiness in living: SOMETHING TO DO, SOMEONE TO LOVE AND SOMETHING TO LOOK FORWARD TO. What are you looking forward to right now?

Stop reading for a few minutes and list ten things you are looking forward to in the next days, weeks, months.

1. _____

2. _____

3. _____

4. _____

5. _____

6. _____

7. _____

8. _____

9. _____

10. _____

If you had a hard time doing it, it might be because you are living in the past and have no plans for your future.

There are three kinds of people when it comes to future planning: THOSE WHO WATCH THINGS HAPPEN, THOSE WHO MAKE THINGS HAPPEN AND THOSE WHO DON'T KNOW WHAT'S HAPPENING. Which one describes you? A person who assumes responsibility for their future is a person who *makes things happen* by constructive and intelligent planning.

YOU CAN FLY BUT
THAT COCOON HAS TO GO!

I am confident that there were many skeptics in the crowd that day as the Wright Brothers announced they were going to fly. Those who had tried in the past had failed. But the Wright Brothers had made their plans and following them proved to everyone that flying for man could be a reality. But in order to become airborne, the Wright brothers had to leave the safety of the ground behind. Flying is only risky when you take your feet off the ground. Assuming responsibility for your future is only risky when you make plans and follow those plans. And perhaps the biggest risk is that the plans might fail.

Edison did not invent the light bulb on the first try. His attempts were fraught with continued failure for months. But success became a reality for him because he did not give up. The secret of success in any area of life is leaving the security of the known and venturing into the unknown. Divorce launches people from a known world into an unknown world. Sometimes divorce will trick you into believing you left your sound mind and good thinking and planning processes in that other world. But you didn't. You still have them and they still work.

I frequently hear the complaint, "I just can't think straight anymore!" "I'm confused, I just can't make decisions." It is difficult to make sound decisions and plans when you are emotionally low. Consult with trusted and wise friends or counselors when you need help in planning.

Divorce can become a cocoon that you can use to hide in from the challenge of the future. You can pull it around you and let it become your excuse for not facing reality. You can only fly if you shed that cocoon.

SETTING REALISTIC GOALS FOR YOURSELF

To list all of the possible goals that a person could set for themselves would fill hundreds of pages. I want to isolate several areas that always seem of paramount importance in a divorce situation. The urgent "big three" that many people struggle with are MONEY, JOB, CAREER or VOCATION. These often emerge as survival goals. Divorce is always expensive and people readily agree that there is not enough money to go around. Jobs may change as a result of the divorce or the need for more money. A non-working spouse may be faced with finding a job in a world where they have no marketable skills. A career or vocation may change or a new one may have to be established. All three of these areas need to be faced realistically. Constructive plans must be made if consistent growth is to be assured.

1. *Evaluate Your Present Situation*

Future planning always begins by looking at your present situation. In the money area it means taking an honest look at income and expenses and the establishing of a workable budget. The hope that someone else will take care of you does not lead to independent growth. Child support and spousal support have ways of disappearing or being very inadequate. Marrying a rich prince or princess is the dream of fairy tales. Living on welfare and food stamps is dependent living and should only be used when necessary. It is demeaning and will cause a loss of self-worth.

A different life-style will dictate a re-evaluation of monetary needs. It may mean acquiring some of the basics in life all over again. Many people in divorce are defeated by losing some of the things they have taken years to build. Things can evaporate and change overnight. Financial security can turn into financial insecurity. It is easy to give up hope. It is hard to begin again.

In the job area, you may be faced with having to find one. If you have not worked for years, you may wonder if you have anything to give in exchange for a paycheck. During a divorce, a persons' self-confidence level is usually very low. Ability to do even a menial job is questioned. It may seem easier to do nothing than to do something.

Explore the possibility of a job that is non-pressure and will help you build the confidence you need for something better down the road. The pay may not be that great and there may be little prestige, but you have to start somewhere. Look upon a first job as a step into your future, not a dead end.

Consult various job placement agencies, take job interest and inventory skills tests to see what jobs you might have natural interest and abilities for. Not knowing what you want to do or be is not an excuse for doing nothing. Every person has talents and abilities. Many are untapped and undiscovered. Become a student of job openings and job opportunities. The career area is where good job planning and growth will eventually lead to. Having a job means you put in time and receive remuneration for that time. Having a career means having identity, prestige, respect and remuneration. You are not just doing something . . YOU ARE SOMETHING!

Careers don't just happen, they are planned. They are not contingent upon circumstances, fate or luck.

Marriage may be the only career or vocation some people have ever had. It may be the only thing they feel they can do. When the marriage dissolved, their career ended.

But marriage is not a career or vocation. It is not the only way to live life. A career is something you discover yourself. You can always have it if you choose to. You can grow in it, expand upon it and receive unlimited satisfaction in doing it.

Remember the question you were asked as a child? "What do you want to be when you grow up?" Most children answer with great dreams and lofty ideals. Some people never get to do what they want because they never make plans and follow them. Others just never grow up.

As you evaluate your present state, look carefully at your money situation, job situation and career destination. Start making plans to get where you want to be. Follow the plans that you make. Be willing to make changes as you go.

2. *Explore New and Potential Situations*

What makes a person an explorer? The thrill of discovering what's around the next bend in the river or on the other side of the mountain.

Children are great explorers. At a young age, their curiosity has not been tempered by the threat of danger. They are thrilled by new discoveries. They want to try all the new things and discover new joys. Then maturity and caution take over and exploration often becomes a threat.

Setting goals for your future will make you an explorer and an adventurer. It will put the thrill of the unknown back into your daily existence.

New situations need not be approached as threatening. Decide that you are exploring and can take what you want and leave what you want. You are considering alternatives.

When you explore a new situation, make a list of the potential positives and negatives of the situation and how each might affect you.

A divorce is like learning to walk all over again. At first you crawl, then you walk (with a little help and support from others) and then you run. Assuming responsibility for your future is setting you free to explore new things, new ideas, new situations.

3. *Establish Short Term and Long Term Goals*

Most of us want things to happen NOW. We don't want to

wait until tomorrow, next week or next year. We fail to set goals for the future because we don't want to wait for the future to arrive. Constructive goal setting is the ability to reach future goals by experiencing the excitement and incentive of short term goals. Let's suppose you wanted to become a shool teacher but you only finished one year of college prior to your marriage. Your long term goal would be becoming a teacher. Your short term goals would involve the steps to attaining that. The first might be enrolling and going back to school. The second short term goal might be getting good grades the first semester to prove you could do it. A third short term goal might be to mentally tune your mind to the new world of academia.

Goals can be set on a day to day basis, week to week, month to month or year to year. They need to be attainable so that you can experience the success and positive reinforcement that they bring. Reaching goals says, "I'M GOING SOMEWHERE." I have a plan and a purpose. Many divorced people bob along through life like corks on the water. They have no plan or purpose and their goals, if any, are largely contingent upon whoever might walk into their life.

Having short term and long term goals will help you get up in the morning excited and go to bed at night satisfied. Your purpose in life will not be tied to another person but to the goals and objectives you have set up for yourself.

4. *Don't Be Afraid of Commitments*

"A marriage ceremony is where promises are made, married life is where they are lived out and a divorce is where they are broken." This is how one person described their life.

Many look back on an unhappy marriage where commitments

76

were not kept and decide that they will never make commitments again. They become "commitment shy" in many of the areas of their life because they have been hurt.

It is easy to build a shrine around your hurt and spend the rest of your days worshipping at it. Broken commitments in your past must not keep you from making new commitments in your future. Past failures do not mean future failures unless we failed to learn from the past. The fear of failing keeps many people from making commitments in the areas of job, career, new responsibilities and new relationships. No one wants to be hurt and no one wants to fail. But the reality of life is that we will be hurt at times and we will fail at times. Growth teaches you how to learn by your experiences. Making any commitment is not easy. It is a decision of the mind and the will. It is lived out by the actions of the person making it. Being a responsible adult means living up to your commitments. Taking responsibility for your future means making a commitment to plan for it.

TEN COMMANDMENTS FOR FORMERLY MARRIEDS

1. THOU SHALT NOT LIVE IN THY PAST.
2. THOU SHALT BE RESPONSIBLE FOR THY PRESENT AND NOT BLAME THY PAST FOR IT.
3. THOU SHALT NOT FEEL SORRY FOR THYSELF INDEFINITELY.
4. THOU SHALT ASSUME THY END OF THE BLAME FOR THY MARRIAGE DISSOLVEMENT.

5. THOU SHALT NOT TRY TO RECONCILE THY PAST AND RECONSTRUCT THY FUTURE BY A QUICK, NEW MARRIAGE.

6. THOU SHALT NOT MAKE THY CHILDREN THE VICTIMS OF THY PAST MARRIAGE.

7. THOU SHALT NOT SPEND ALL THY TIME TRYING TO CONVINCE THY CHILDREN HOW TERRIBLE AND EVIL THEIR DEPARTED PARENT IS.

8. THOU SHALT LEARN ALL THOU CAN ABOUT BEING A ONE PARENT FAMILY AND GET ON WITH IT.

9. THOU SHALT ASK OTHERS FOR HELP WHEN THOU NEEDEST IT.

10. THOU SHALT ASK GOD FOR THE WISDOM TO BURY YESTERDAY, CREATE TODAY AND PLAN FOR TOMORROW.

5. *Trust God With Your Future*

In the Ten Commandments for Formerly Married Persons, the tenth commandment is "Thou shalt ask God for the wisdom to bury yesterday, create today and plan for tomorrow."

Trusting God with your future is inviting God to direct your conscious thoughts and plans as you set goals and objectives for your future. It is asking God for His wisdom in your planning and projecting. It is living with the confidence that God is in charge of your life today and He will be in charge of tomorrow too. Trusting God with your future does not mean you fail to plan for it. Some people do nothing and hope God will do everything. God has given you a mind to use. He does not expect us to be inane robots who never think and act only upon command. The scriptures tell us in II Timothy 1:7 that "God has not given us the spirit of fear, but of power and love and of a sound mind." God expects us to use our sound mind in planning and setting goals for our future.

Trusting God with your future does not mean that it will be free of troubles and problems. It does mean that you have someone to take the troubles and problems to when they happen. It does not always mean that you will like what is happening but it does mean you can trust God with what is happening.

Your future can be your friend or your enemy. You can move creatively and constructively toward it by formulating goals and objectives. It's your future. Plan ahead . . . you have to live there!

PERSONAL GROWTH AND DISCUSSION QUESTIONS

1. Discuss what goals you would like to set for yourself in the following areas:

   MONEY

   JOB

   CAREER

2. Develop a series of 7 to 10 goals for yourself for the next 3 to 6 months.

1. _____

2. _____

3. _____

4. _____

5. _____

6. _____

7. _____

8. _____

9. _____

10. _____

3. If you knew that you could not fail, what would you attempt to do?

4. What are the biggest problems you have in setting and reaching your goals?

5. Discuss honestly, how you feel right now about your future.

6. My personal goal for this next week is

_____

_____

_____

_____

_____

**GROWING
THROUGH
DIVORCE**

7

FINDING A FAMILY

"Having a family means you belong to someone."

Contemporary society has two largely distinctive traits. It is couple oriented and family inclined. As I am writing this, it is the month of June and as a minister, I will perform a number of weddings during this month. All of these weddings will involve a man and a woman joining together in the sharing of wedding vows and commitments. In the eyes of the state, God, family and friends, they will officially become "couples." For many of them, a natural outgrowth of that coupling process will be the bearing of children. Two people are a couple. Two people with a child or children is a family.

If the above is true, would it be logical to say that if one mate or the other leaves the family through divorce, it is not a family anymore? No, I don't think so. But many of us think of family only in a generic sense or a living-together sense.

Having a family means you belong to someone! You have a supportive group of people around you that accept you, care about you, love you and support you.

Divorce uproots and dismembers families. It can cause the members of that family to feel family-less. It is vitally important that a sense of family and support are maintained through divorce.

I want to share with you in this chapter, three kinds of families and how a sense of knowing you belong to a family can help you grow through divorce.

The Family You Were Born Into

The first family that you became aware of was the family that you were born into. It probably consisted of a mother, father, brothers, sisters, along with other relatives. No one consulted you while you were a struggling embryo and asked you what family you wanted to be born into. You had no choice in the matter whatever. And once you arrived into that family, the family itself had no choice on whether or not to keep you or send you back for a different model. You were there and they were there. They had to begin accepting you and you had to begin accepting them. They made you feel loved, wanted and comfortable long before you could exchange that same feeling for them.

Many of the thoughts and feelings about family that you have today probably came as a result of your experiences in the family you were born into and grew up in. Looking back, you may assess some of those experiences as good and some as bad—some as negative and some as positive. Regardless of your feelings, it was your earthly family and it brought you into this life.

Reflecting back on your earthly family, think about these four questions for a few minutes.

1. How does or did that family receive you?
2. How did you or do you receive it?
3. What did it do for you?
4. What did you do for it?

Your earthly family was your introduction to people on this earth. From it you either found support and love or you were denied it. Hopefully, you gave something to it and it gave something to you.

The Family That You Married Into

With family and friends around you, you stood one day at a new point in your life. You made the decision to marry and establish a new family. In order to do this, you left the old one behind and placed your priorities and attentions in the new one. You did not abandon the old family, you added, by choice a new one. It started with two people, and perhaps quicker than you wanted, it became three. It was your family, you created it by your choice. You dreamed your dreams and set your goals.

You injected into it all that you had learned from your own family. In looking back on this second family in your life, think about these questions for a few minutes.

1. What dreams do you or did you have for this family?
2. Have those dreams been fulfilled?
3. Do you still feel a part of that family?
4. Do you feel family-less since your divorce?

The family that you married into may not have fulfilled your expectations. Your divorce may have left you disenchanted with the whole idea of family. It may have embittered you and left you looking for a family that would not change by whim or with a change of mind. You may be questioning the whole concept of a family right now and wondering if you can ever feel the love, warmth and support of one again.

The family that you were born into can be taken from you through death. You can move away from the old home, family and friends. Distance can lessen the importance that family plays in your life. Divorce can cause you to lose the family you married into and sometimes, because of feelings and misunderstandings, your natural family may become very remote in your life as well.

The experience of losing family after having it can be traumatic. The struggle to regain a sense of family and identify with one is even more difficult.

God's Family

In our ministry to divorced persons at Garden Grove Community Church, we teach people that there is a third family that they can become a part of. This family is the family of God.

If you are reading this book and you have had little or no experience with God in your life, it may seem strange to you to think about the family of God in a sense of personal belonging. You may not see it as taking the place of an earthly family. Let me share with you some distinctives about the family of God that you may never have thought of.

1. God's family is a "Forever Family." It is permanent and unchanging. It is unlike your earthly family or your marriage family. You can lose them by death, distance, deed or divorce. Once you decide to become a part of God's family, you are a member for all time and eternity. In I Peter 2, verses 9 and 10, there is a promise concerning this: "But you are a chosen race, a royal priesthood, a holy nation, a people for God's own possession, that you may proclaim the excellencies of Him who has called you out of darkness into His marvelous light; for once you were not a people, but now you are the people of God; you had not received mercy, but now you have received mercy."

2. You can join God's family by receiving and recognizing His son, Jesus Christ, as the new director of your life. When you were a child, one of the first words you learned to speak was Da-Da. As you grew older it became Daddy, then perhaps Dad or Father. You slowly came to associate that name with love, correction, caring, instruction, provision, protection. The longer you knew him, the more Dad meant in your life. You learned to recognize him while you were very young. You received him into your growing life because you understood that he cared for you and loved you.

The very same principle is true when you give your life to Christ. You learn to trust Him and love Him because He daily shows those same things to you. You build a relationship with Him in a day-by-day walk with Him. He means something to you and you mean something to HIM.

3. You grow each day that you are a part of this family. Many people who decide to become a part of God's family have many questions. There are many things they wonder about and don't know.

Growth and knowledge are only achieved as we live each day. When a person decides to follow Christ and be a part of God's family, he needs to learn everything he can about the person he is following and about how that family functions. Some of this comes by study, worship, prayer, and talking to other members of the family. It comes slowly but surely and in much the same way that growth came about as you learned more about your earthly father and what he expected from you.

God is never in a hurry. He has lots of time. He would like to walk beside you and help you in your journey through life.

4. When you join the family of God, you join as a brother or sister and you inherit all the others who have joined before you as your new brothers and sisters. That's joining a pretty large family! There is no larger family in existence than God's family. What a sense of belonging that can give you. You may feel alone, empty, friendless and family-less. But when you join the family of God, you have instant family and a supportive fellowship that will accept you as you are and struggle with you and grow with you. They will be with you in the happy moments as well as the sad ones. They will extend a love to you

that will be beyond even that of your own families at times. Joining the family of God is joining the "loving bunch" as someone recently described them.

5. You have responsibilities to all the other members in this family just as they have responsibilities to you. Remember when your father or mother assigned you your first chores. You really thought you were somebody. For years you had mimicked the jobs your parents did in your play world. Finally they assigned you some real jobs and you zealously went about them each day—until they became routine, mundane and boring. Then you tried to avoid them. But somehow it never quite worked and you still had to do them. You had a job to uphold your end of the family's responsibilities.

Don't mistake this kind of responsibility with what we were speaking about in the other chapters. I said that you were not responsible *for* other people and their actions. In the family of God, you are responsible *to* other members in living out with them the Christian life-style. You are responsible to:

ACCEPT THEM AS BROTHERS AND SISTERS
ACCEPT THEM AS THEY ARE
SHARE YOUR LIFE WITH THEM
LOVE THEM AND SUPPORT THEM
HELP THEM WHEN POSSIBLE
AFFIRM THEM WITH THE LOVE OF CHRIST

They, in return are responsible to care for you in the same way. The Apostle Paul put it in these words, "Therefore encourage one another, and build up one another, just as you also are doing." (I Thessalonians 5:11)

6. You can't "unjoin" this family. There are many ways of

losing relationships with your earthly family. There are many ways of breaking relationships with the family you married into. Divorce is one of those ways. A lawyer, a piece of paper and a pronouncement by a judge. And it's all over. How does a person get a divorce from God? Is there such a thing? I don't believe there is. The scripture states these words by Jesus, "And the one who comes to me I will certainly not cast out." (John 6:37)

Once we come to God and give our life to Christ, we receive the promise that God will not cast us away or turn His back on us. This does not mean that we cannot or will not turn our back on Him. We can drift from God by our own choice. We can shrug off our responsibilities to grow and have a relationship with God in name only. That would be comparable to having family privileges without family responsibilities.

Many people who have gone through a divorce have lost the warmth and closeness of family. They lack a supportive community of people around them who genuinely care about them and what happens to them. An indispensable part of our successful program for formerly married persons is helping people care for people. This is accomplished by letting people know that there is a place in our midst where they can find acceptance, caring and love. They are welcomed into a group of people who have shared in similar experiences and who have discovered for themselves that life does not end at divorce. Through small group discussion programs, seminars, workshops, personal counseling and biblical teaching, many people who are left with the feeling that no one cares, find in reality that many people here really do care. Help is given in bringing the formerly married back to emotional strength and health. Practical assistance is given in meeting the every day demands of making life work. A strong spirit of family is in evidence as the members of our varied age groups intermingle in the areas of mental, social, physical and spiritual growth each week.

The spirit that pervades our ministry to the formerly married is the spirit of Christ. It is the spirit of acceptance and forgiveness that we will speak about in the next chapter. There are people who care deeply about you and want you to know the love that they know by being a part of the family of God. These words describe how some join our family and God's family:

I CAME SEARCHING

Out of my lonely place,
  I came searching.
Out of my hidden fears,
  I came searching.
Out of my need for friends,
  I came searching.
Out of my quest for God,
  I came searching.
And I found a people who care,
  And a new love to share.

HOW CAN I FIND A SUPPORTIVE FELLOWSHIP?

Making a commitment of your life to Christ and joining God's family is the key part of a new beginning for you. Once you have reached this decision it is important that you become a part of a group of people who have shared your experience and are trying to go in the same direction as you are.

There are many good groups across the country that will fill your days with mental, social and physical pursuits geared to the divorced person. There are very few that offer fellowship and support in the spiritual area. The agency in our world that can and should offer help in all four areas is the church. Many churches, however, frown upon having divorced persons in their midst while others simply do not see the need for it.

Make an appointment with a minister you might know or one who might be receptive to you and explore the possibility of starting a group to minister to the needs of the formerly married persons in your community. Once the word gets out that you are offering an alternative to the bar scene, you will have people climbing the walls to get in and share in an authentic fellowship that has a purpose in being.

It's not easy but the rewards of ministering to the needs of formerly married persons are immensely satisfying. I can speak from personal experience for that is my job.

PERSONAL GROWTH AND DISCUSSION QUESTIONS

1. Describe the kind of relationship you have today with the family that you were born into.

2. How did your family feel about your divorce?

3. How did your divorce affect your concepts and feelings about family?

4. If you have a supportive family around you, describe how you feel about it and how it helps you.

5. Have you become a member of God's "Forever Family"? If you have, describe how that happened to you.

6. My personal growth goal for this week is

_____

_____

_____

_____

_____

GROWING
THROUGH
DIVORCE

8

FINDING AND
EXPERIENCING FORGIVENESS

"I'm not perfect, I'm just forgiven!"

In the recovery process of working through a divorce, there is an area that many people are reluctant to deal with. It is the area of finding and experiencing forgiveness. A person can learn to deal with the many aspects of being divorced on a mechanical level but the area of forgiveness must be dealt with on a spiritual level.

In the religious community, divorce has stood for a long time as the somewhat unforgivable sin. The Bible does not teach this but the church has somehow convinced a lot of people that it does. Divorce often becomes a worse sin than stealing or murder. A divorced person is looked upon as permanently marred, bruised, tainted or condemned. Although these viewpoints seem very medieval and un-Christlike, they are experienced by many people who have gone through a divorce.

Our purpose in this chapter is not to change the attitude of the religious community toward the divorced person. That is slowly happening in many areas. Whether or not the religious community or your church forgives you is not that important. What is important is that you know and experience personal forgiveness.

FORGIVENESS GETS THE HATE OUT

I don't know of any other experience in life outside of divorce that can stretch a person's emotions and feelings from love to hate.

Divorce can cause you to build walls in your life in place of bridges. You can start out by hating an ex-spouse and end-up by hating yourself and everyone around you. You can literally drown yourself in a sea of negative feelings towards others and yourself. This kind of emotional bath can keep you from growing and becoming a new person.

Time diminishes hate but it does not heal it. Experiencing forgiveness gets the hate out of your life permanently. There are several areas in knowing forgiveness that I would like to share with you.

GOD FORGIVES ME!

I believe that one of the greatest therapies that God ever gave to man was the therapy of forgiveness. Without it, we would live in a constant state of guilt that could never be removed. Jesus set the stage for this in the scriptures. In the Gospel of John, chapter 8, Jesus is confronted with some religious leaders of His day who have brought a woman to him. The charge is that she was caught in the act of adultery. You will not read very far in this chapter before you will decide that the religious leaders were bent upon exacting punishment while Jesus was concerned about enacting forgiveness to the woman. In the last verse of this biblical incident, Jesus speaks to the woman with these words, "Neither do I condemn you; go your way; from now on sin no more."

What I see happening here sets an example of how we can look at other people's mistakes and how God deals with those mistakes. Jesus did not penalize the woman. He forgave her and encouraged her to begin living a new kind of life.

The religious leaders would have made an example of her to others. Jesus understood man's humanity and imperfections far better than those who were supposed to be the priests to men.

The scriptures contain numerous accounts of how Jesus dealt with human weakness. He expressed disappointment at it many times but he never condemned it. He was in the forgiveness business. In response to the disciples' request for an example of prayer, Jesus included the words "Forgive us our trespasses as we forgive those who trespass against us." Forgiveness is reciprocal. In the First Epistle of John, chapter 1, verse 9, we read, "If we confess our sin, He is faithful and righteous to forgive us our sins and to cleanse us from all unrighteousness." This verse is a promise that lets us know we can be forgiven if we admit our sin.

I believe divorce is a sin. It was not a part of God's perfect plan for man. But man in his weakness and humanity cannot always live up to God's ideal. The standards for man are set by God. When man breaks the standard, he must have a way to experience God's forgiveness and be restored to fellowship with God.

Dr. Dwight Small in an article entitled, "Divorce and Remarriage: A Fresh Biblical Perspective" states; "All divorce is failure to meet God's standard and hence it is sin; all parties alike need God's grace. But to all divorced Christians, guilty as well as innocent, renewing grace is available. The sole condition is true penitence, confession, and the sincere desire to go on to fulfill God's purpose."

Experiencing God's forgiveness begins by confession of our weakness and wrongdoing.

Remember when you were a child and you disobeyed your parents. Perhaps you covered it up for a time and they did not know about it. But you knew and you lived with the threat of being discovered and punished. Added to that was the weight of a guilty conscience. When you finally confessed your wrongdoing, you experienced a great sense of relief and the good feeling that everything was all right again between you and your parents.

The same good feeling prevails when we make things right with God. Here is a simple prayer that may express how you feel. Take a moment and share it with God.

God, I know that divorce is wrong.
I know it was not your ideal for me.
God, I confess to you my weaknesses

98

and human failings that contributed
knowingly and unknowingly to my divorce.
God, I ask your forgiveness for my divorce.
Help me to know and experience your love
through your forgiveness.
Lead me to new growth and new beginnings
in my life.
Thank you Lord!   Amen.

I FORGIVE ME!

The second part of experiencing forgiveness is the most difficult for many people. It is easier to confess our humanity before God than it is to admit it to ourselves. We live by the motto: "I'M NOT PERFECT, BUT JUST DON'T REMIND ME OF IT." It is extremely hard to admit our own weaknesses and shortcomings.

The finest court in the land could not examine all the intricacies that combined to cause a marriage to fail. Few counselors are skilled enough to assess who or what caused the marriage to disintegrate. Lacking a pronouncement of some form that would place the blame, many people who go through a divorce take the blame upon themselves. Others might tend to absolve themselves of all blame.

Many people who experience divorce cannot forgive themselves for whatever part they played in the process. They end up playing the game of "IF ONLY I'D . . . ." There is no way you can win this game because you can't change anything. What has happened is history.

Forgiving yourself means:
    I ACCEPT MY HUMANITY AS A HUMAN BEING

I HAVE THE FREEDOM TO FAIL
I ACCEPT RESPONSIBILITY FOR MY FAILURES
I CAN FORGIVE MYSELF FOR MY FAILURES
I ACCEPT GOD'S FORGIVENESS
I CAN BEGIN AGAIN

Many people live under the yoke of self-imposed guilt. They are unable to accept the fact that to be human means you will make mistakes. Until they can experience the refreshing climate of self-forgiveness, they will not enjoy their humanity.

I FORGIVE MY EX-SPOUSE

I can hear you saying, "Now that's carrying things too far! After all that he or she has done to me, I will never forgive them."

When a person is caught in the heat of argument and emotional combat, forgiveness is usually the very last thing to come to mind. Be aware that forgiveness is not an instant thing but a process that you grow into. Few people that I have shared these thoughts with in Divorce Growth Seminars have raced out of the class to see if they work. Forgiveness from God comes easiest and is the first step. Self-forgiveness is second and is a little harder. Forgiveness in the ex-spouse realm is usually a long way down the recovery road and can only happen when the fires of divorce cool long enough to let sound thinking take over.

A person asked me recently what to say to an ex-spouse in this area. You might start by saying, "I'm sorry. I ask your forgiveness for all my mistakes and whatever part I might have played in contributing to our divorce." Sounds hard doesn't it?

It is. But the personal sense of growth and well being that comes from doing it makes it worthwhile.

Asking forgiveness of an ex-spouse is admitting your weaknesses and the contributions you made to the divorce. It is saying that you were a part of the marriage and a part of the divorce. It is also recognizing the worth of another person and that they are forgivable.

Many post divorce relationships remain hostile and tense for years. Forgiving an ex-spouse means asking forgiveness for your wrongs and also giving forgiveness to the ex-spouse for their wrongs. Remember, you are only accountable for yourself. It is not your job to remind others of their wrongs so that they can ask you to forgive them.

MY EX-SPOUSE FORGIVES ME

What if they don't? You have just put yourself on the line and asked for forgiveness. The response may not have been what you hoped for. Forgiveness was refused, treated lightly, laughed at or just ignored. What do you do now? Nothing! You have fulfilled your part of the responsibility. You cannot elicit or control the responses you want from other people. If they choose to ignore you, then you must let it be their problem. You can be confident that you have done all that you can and the rest is up to them.

FORGIVING AND FORGETTING

I have listened to many people tell me that they can forgive but they will never forget. And I would agree that, on their own strength, forgetting will be hard if not impossible. I believe that the forgetting of things must be left up to God. We all know that time is a healer and time causes us to forget. As tensions and hurts are erased through seeking forgiveness, I believe we slowly forget the bad things and remember the good. You can always take personal action in the forgiveness realm. You will have to trust God and time with the forgetting area.

God is in the business of introducing people to new beginnings. His method of doing this is to bring healing and wholeness into lives through struggle and growth.

The scripture teaches unlimited forgiveness. In Matthew 18:22 in the New Testament, Jesus states that we forgive "seventy times seven." That does not mean we forgive four hundred ninety times and quit. It means that God's forgiveness and ours should be unlimited.

Divorce can be shattering and devastating but it is not unforgivable. I believe that God looks upon the millions of lives that have been deeply wounded by divorce and wants to bring into those lives the fresh breezes of His love and forgiveness.

IT CAN HAPPEN TO YOU! You won't be perfect but you will be forgiven!

PRAYER FOR THE DIVORCED

God, Master of Union and Disunion,
Teach me how I may now walk
Alone and strong.
Heal my wounds;
Let the scar tissue of Thy bounty
Cover these bruises and hurts
That I may again be a single person
Adjusted to new days.
Grant me a heart of wisdom,
Cleanse me of hostility, revenge and rancor,
Make me know the laughter which is not giddy,
The affection which is not frightened.
Keep far from me thoughts of evil and despair.
May I realize that the past chapter of my life
Is closed and will not open again.
The anticipated theme of my life has changed,
The expected story end will not come.
Shall I moan at the turn of the plot?
Rather, remembering without anger's thrust
Recalling without repetitive pain of regret,
Teach me again to write and read
That I may convert this unexpected epilogue
Into a new preface and a new poem.
Muddled gloom over,
Tension days passed,
Let bitterness of thought fade
Harshness of memory attenuate
Make me move on in love and kindness.

                                    (Source Unknown)

PERSONAL GROWTH AND DISCUSSION QUESTIONS

1. If you have experienced God's forgiveness in your divorce, describe how this came about and what brought you to it.

2. Where are you in the struggle to forgive yourself?

3. If you have asked your ex-spouse for forgiveness, what happened? If you have not, how do you feel about doing it?

4. Describe an experience from your life where you wanted forgiveness and received or did not receive it.

5. How are you handling the ''forgetting'' in your divorce?

6. My personal growth goal for this week is

_____

_____

_____

_____

_____

GROWING
THROUGH
DIVORCE

9

THIRTY-SEVEN GOING
ON SEVENTEEN

*"I resent . . . having to act, think and date
like a seventeen year old again."*

A person's social existence is drastically altered by divorce. The divorced person no longer seems to fit the world of the married. Social contacts and social calendars change abruptly when people separate. A divorced person is tossed from the security of always having a special someone there to having no one there. If they intend to continue socializing in the human race, they are forced to go out with members of the same sex or they are forced to go to bars, clubs and singles groups and compete for the attention of members of the opposite sex. The singles world can be a scary world and can send you running back to the security of your home or apartment. Little wonder that so many singles are in hiding.

In a recent conversation, a divorced person shared this comment with me: "I resent being thirty-seven years of age and having to act, think and date like a seventeen year old again." Most formerly married people that I meet share those sentiments. And yet, if a person is to have a social life, meet new friends and establish new relationships, they will have to date.

Some people coming out of a divorce decide to jump right into the dating game and try to quickly establish a new relationship that leads to a new marriage. They are propelled by their own insecurity and fear of being alone. It is a mistake to jump into any kind of relationship until you have had time to adjust to your divorce and the new demands it has placed upon you.

BUILDING A NEW RELATIONSHIP . . . THE FEARS

There are six questions that I hear people ask as they consider building a new relationship with the opposite sex.

1. *Can I be sure it will last this time?*

There are a very few guarantees in relationships. It is very easy to be on the defensive and be relationship-shy after going through a divorce. Some are so hurt by the divorce that they fend off any new relationships even after a long period of time fearing the same end in a new relationship. All a person can do is learn from the experiences they have had in the past and walk hopefully and trustingly into the future.

2. *Can I ever trust another man or woman again?*

All people are not the same. If you are hurt or lose trust in one person, it does not mean that everyone will treat you the same. All men are not bad. All women are not bad. It is very unfair to develop a distrust of the opposite sex in general just because of a bad experience you have had. Trust grows over a period of time. Lasting relationships don't develop overnight. Some formerly marrieds want instant friendships or marriages without developing trust levels.

3. *Will I make the same mistakes again?*

Not if you learn by them and give yourself time to grow. It generally takes a person from one to two years to get a perspective on their divorce and learn the needed lessons from it. In sports, good coaching and good practice eliminates bad habits and mistakes. An honest evaluation of the mistakes you might have made in your marriage will help you learn from them. Blaming the other party will not help you learn anything. Facing your mistakes honestly will help you learn. Most people learn by trial and error. Most will admit the trials but too few admit the errors. If you don't correct your mistakes, you will take them into another marriage and make them all over again.

4. *Can I be happy if I marry again?*

People have been trying to define happiness for years. It means different things to different people. Many people look for that special person to make them happy. They don't want to assume the responsibility for themselves. They want someone else to assume it. Happy people attract happy people. Happiness is more internal than external. If you work on your own happiness level, you will take happiness into a new relationship. Being married does not insure happiness any more than being single does.

5. *What if I don't find someone?*

National statistics indicate that ninety percent of all divorced persons remarry. With the averages on your side, the chances are very likely that you will remarry some day. Hopefully you will wait until you can put your life back together and grow from the experience of your divorce. Women frequently ask where all the good, eligible men are. The men ask where all the good eligible women are. One thing is for sure—they are not all hiding in the same place. There are good people everywhere. You will find them if you take the time to look.

There are some people who will choose not to remarry and this is a personal choice. Not everyone should be married and not everyone should be single. Every individual should evaluate for themselves what is best for them.

6. *Will I feel confident and sure enough to begin dating?*

It is not easy to start a dating life after being married for fifteen, twenty, or twenty-five years. In many instances, it's not a case of being too old, but too rusty. Remembering what to say, what to do, where to go, how to act is not easy when you have lived a long time with only one person. Dating after many years of a married existence will be as scary for you as it is for your fourteen year old son or daughter. You build confidence as you go. And unless you decide to remain single the rest of your life, you will have to enter the dating world.

BUILDING A NEW RELATIONSHIP . . . THE CAUTIONS

There are always some caution flags to be raised in the world of post divorce dating. The following questions will help you examine some of the cautions.

1. *Have I learned anything about ME through my divorce?*

Everyone should write their own short book bearing the title, "Lessons My Divorce Has Taught Me." The opening chapters should deal with the things you have learned about yourself. Part of the growth process in divorce is learning who you are. If you jump into post divorce dating without evaluating what you have learned about yourself, your strengths and weaknesses, you might be setting yourself up for another fall. For a person in their first post divorce dating relationship, there is a great risk that if that relationship does not end in marriage, they will suffer the same emotional shock upon a breakup as they did in their divorce. Take some time to evaluate what you have learned about yourself through your divorce.

2. *Has enough time elapsed to let the dust settle?*

Previously we mentioned that it takes from one to two years for the dust to settle in most peoples' lives, depending upon how long you were married. Proving to an ex-mate that you are still desirable by a quick new marriage won't help that dust to settle. Give yourself all the time you need and then some. The greatest mistake of divorced persons is to remarry too quickly.

3. *Am I building healthy relationships?*

A good marriage is one where both parties are interdependent of each other. A healthy relationship is not a leaning one where one person drains the other. Each person has to contribute something in the building of a healthy relationship. In a healthy relationship, there is a balance between giving and receiving. A good rule would be to date people who are at least as far removed from their divorce as you are. They will have had time to get their own life in order.

In many singles groups, there are people who prey upon emotionally weaker people to meet their own ego needs. No matter how shakey you feel on the emotional level, avoid these people like the plague. A healthy relationship can be established when both parties are growing and have come to terms with their own divorce.

4. *How much of my past marriage am I dragging into my new relationship?*

You will know you are gaining in your own growth and post divorce adjustment when you talk less and less about your former marriage, spouse and divorce. People who are recovering from their divorce usually don't want to keep hearing divorce stories. If you spend your dating hours rehashing your divorce, you are dragging excess baggage along with you. If you don't get it behind you, you may bring it with you into a new marriage. Leave the past in the past and concentrate on new beginnings with new goals and new dreams.

BUILDING A NEW RELATIONSHIP . . . THE TRUSTS

The sign on the wall said, "In God we trust, all others pay cash." It conveyed the level of trust that the restaurant owners had with their clientele. It is easy to trust God. He has a good track record. It is usually harder to trust people because they can let you down.

In the world of relationships, each of us has some kind of relationship with God, with ourselves and with the people around us. Each day we work at building those relationships.

Divorce shatters these relationships and causes us to doubt their security and validity. Building new relationships begins with the help of God in the following areas.

1. *With my trust in God and with His help, I can begin again.*

Building England from the ruins after the severe bombings in World War II was a major job. Without the undying determination of the British people, England would still be in ruins. Building a life when it appears in ruin is not easy and it will take the best determination you can find. God is not in the business of applauding your failures. He wants you to put your trust in Him and be about the business of new beginnings.

2. *With the help of God, I can learn to love and trust in new ways.*

Love and trust sometimes evaporate completely during a divorce. Rebuilding them becomes a mammoth undertaking. The fear of loving again and being hurt may cause you to give up trying. Bertrand Russell said, "To fear love is to fear life and those who fear life are already three parts dead." You may feel dead but you are alive. With the daily help of God you will learn to love and trust in new ways.

3. *I will trust that God is doing a new work in my life and will continue to do it. If and when I remarry, it will be the richest experience of my life.*

Remarriage for some people is an option while for others it is an opportunity. If God is at work in your life, it will be a great opportunity.

At our church, an exciting group of people meet for study and fellowship each week. They all have one thing in common; they have been married before. They all walked through the valley of divorce and struggled up the mountain of recovery on the other side. They know the hurt, the heartache, the loneliness that divorce can bring. But they were not defeated by it. They worked at rebuilding their lives by forming new relationships. Those relationships have led to marriage and a rich new experience for these people. They share their struggles, joys and pain as they work to make their marriages work. The next chapter will deal with some of the problems they face.

The dating, relating and mating of divorced persons can be one of the most difficult areas that you may face in growing through your divorce. You may alternately run to it and run from it. You may despair of so many dates and relationships that seem meaningless. You may feel like a piece of merchandise in an open air market. But don't let what you feel influence what you are. You are on the way to rebuilding your life. Day-by-day you are putting new blocks into place. God is doing a new work in your life and will continue to do it.

PERSONAL GROWTH AND DISCUSSION QUESTIONS

1. List some of the personal fears that you have in thinking about building a new relationship.

2. What have you learned about yourself at this stage of your divorce?

3. Describe the person you married the first time and the kind of person you would like to marry in the future.

4. What role is God playing in your life as you think about building a new relationship?

5. My personal growth goal for this week is

_____

_____

_____

_____

_____

GROWING THROUGH DIVORCE

10

REMARRIAGE —— YOURS, MINE AND MAYBE OUR FAMILIES

"When I got married I was looking for an ideal,
Then it became an ordeal,
Now I want a new deal."

Finding a "new deal" in remarriage is not always easy. If divorce has its spectrum of problems and frustrations, remarriage has its own challenges to all who enter in. Many people who find a new relationship that results in marriage seem to feel that things will be just as they were in their previous marriage. The only difference will be the new spouse. It does not take very long to find out that remarriage places a person in a whole new world with added complications to daily routines. A remarriage is not simply a union between two people as it might have been the first time. It is also a union between two different families, and if both ex-spouses have remarried, it could well be a union between four different families. It could double your pleasure and quadruple your frustrations.

Working out the intricacies of two and four family living takes time and there are a number of things to consider and think through both prior to and after remarriage.

POST REMARRIAGE CONSIDERATIONS

1. How many children will be directly involved in the marriage, who will have custody, who will support them and where will they live? Because we are speaking about unknown situations here, we will not try to answer the questions but merely ask them and let you wrestle with them.
2. How much money of the new family's income will go to support the ex-spouse and children?
3. Where will you live—his house, your house or a new house? Many hurts are spared when new housing is provided. This avoids anyone being a guest in another person's home.
4. How will the children address their new parents?
5. Where will children who live with ex-spouses stay when they come for weekends, vacations or overnight?
6. What about legal adoptions and name changes for the children?
7. How will the discipline be handled in the home? Will favoritism be shown to one mate's children over the others?

116

These are just a few of the many things that come up when children are involved in remarriage. If children are grown and married, the problems may move to the grandfather-grandmother level. A list of potential problems should be made prior to remarriage and thoroughly discussed. Waiting until the problems occur will not enhance the happiness of a new marriage.

Three things that never seem to be totally resolved in most remarriages are the ongoing relationship with the former spouse, the fair and even treatment of the children on both sides and the constant strain of stretching the family budget over two households.

From my experience of working with formerly married persons who enter new marriages, the following things will need attention and resolving if the marriage is to be successful.

WHO SHOULD YOU BE LOYAL TO?

Present spouse? Former spouse? Your own children? Your inherited children? On the surface, the answer might be quite obvious to you. But life is lived out where the little things are faced on an hour to hour basis. Loyalties that are clearly thought out may change with new circumstances. If your ex-spouse were critically ill in another state, would you drop everything and run to their bedside? If your new mate exacts severe discipline on YOUR children, will your loyalty be to him or her or to the children? If your children seem to be getting in the way and trying to wreck your new marriage, where will your loyalties be placed?

Parents need to support each other and stand with each other. Many children try to wreck a new marriage by playing one parent against the other. Some might simply want their own parent back and feel very resentful and hostile to the new substitute parent. Spending time talking with the children prior to the marriage will be helpful. Any child will wonder about the role of a new parent coming into the home. Will they be kind, harsh, loving, mean? They want to know how their lives will be affected by this new relationship. A first family has a chance to grow into things. A second family is thrown into things. Too many times discussions and decisions come after the fact. The time to discuss loyalties on all levels is before they are challenged.

HOW TO WIN WITH STEPCHILDREN

No one can become an instant father or mother overnight. It is going to take time and adjustment on everyone's part. Many new parents simply expect stepchildren to welcome them with open arms and keep living as though nothing had happened. Few children make an easy adjustment, especially if their real parent is close by and in contact with them. The first rule for success as a stepparent is to give the new relationship time to grow and develop.

The second step would be to really work at building that relationship. Your new position in the home may grant you authority but respect is something you earn. I feel that the responsibility is on the shoulders of the new parent to work at winning the respect and love of the stepchildren. A child may resent a new parent for showing love and affection for his mother or father when little of that love is shown to him. I have known stepparents who have literally ignored their stepchildren and left them entirely up to the natural parent. Few homes will survive this kind of cold treatment.

A third step in winning with stepchildren is to make them feel as important as your own natural children. A love that is shared equally will bring great returns. There are a million ways a stepparent can share and show love. Love always wins.

A fourth step is to realize that you are not a replacement for the other parent. Don't try to be. You are who you are and not a replica of the departed parent. Don't get trapped into playing the role and letting yourself be compared with the absent father or mother. Affirm your own individuality from the beginning and you will gain respect.

HOW TO ADJUST TO DIFFERENT LIFE-STYLES

In remarriage, children have to adjust to and compete with different life-styles. One life-style is maintained in the weekday home where they live while a quite different life-style may be lived when they visit their weekend parent. If the weekend parent has not remarried, visitations may be an endless round of entertainment and funmaking. Discipline may be totally abandoned. The return to reality on Sunday evening can be quite traumatic and it may take several days for the child to adjust to their weekday home.

Separated parents need to work at coordinating life-styles for the children that will not have great variances in them. If the weekend parent has remarried, an honest effort should be put forth to make the weekend an extension of the week rather than an interference or climax to the child's week. Many parents fail to realize that they put their children on emotional roller coasters by failing to strive for some continuity in schedules, disciplines, entertainments and acceptance. Too many parents think only of themselves and the children become an addendum to their life-styles.

When cooperation is lacking in the other parent to maintain a smooth flow in the children's life-style, it would be helpful to explain to the child what is really going on and why. Children can understand many things if time is taken for the explanation.

People have a right to live as they choose to live but only so far as that freedom is not an infringement upon the healthy growth of another person.

HOW TO TREAT YOUR SPOUSE'S EX-MATE

In an earlier chapter, we referred to the fact that divorce is unlike death because it leaves the ex-mate hovering about the fringes of the broken relationship. Prior to a remarriage by one or both parties, there usually is a constant barrage of nit-picking and disagreeing on everything under the sun. When one party remarries, the tensions begin to lessen somewhat due to the diversion of having to turn attentions in another direction. When both parties remarry, the tension usually begins to disappear completely as both parties have their time well filled with other things.

It is at this point that healthy relationships can be built with ex-mates. This may appear to be an ideal to some or want to be just avoided by others. The need to have a smooth relationship with an ex-mate is extremely important if you have children. Emotional wars take a high toll of a person's well being and stability. The ideal in any divorce situation is to end up having the ex-mate as a friend. It is easier to live around a friend than an enemy.

A new mate can help you develop a growing relationship with your ex-spouse by helping you see things objectively. We all need people who act as interpreters and facilitators in our life. They help us explore what is being said and done by seeing that we keep our psychological distance. They can assume the role of sounding board and emotional buffer for us.

A new mate can also develop a hospitable friendship with your ex-spouse. This will probably only happen if he or she is very secure within themselves.

We all have to learn in life to work with other people. We cannot always run from those who are difficult. It is doubtful that a high social and friendship level will be desired or reached in ex-mate remarriage structures. An honest goal would be to have a relationship that is devoid of hostility and open to honest communication as is needed.

If communication is open and honest, positive construction will take place in the lives of the children and parents. It is a high ideal but well worth aiming for.

HOW TO RELATE TO IN-LAWS, OUTLAWS AND OTHER FRIENDS

Some remarriages will cause you to acquire a whole new world of friends and relatives while others will cause you to lose them. Your family and friends may not agree with your choice and discontinue their relationships with you. Others will be supportive and continue friendships. A remarriage will place you in a whole new world as far as family and friends are concerned. There is very little you can say or do if people exclude you as a friend or relative. In all likelihood you will win a few and lose a few. A good guideline here would be to work at keeping the friendships you value and let the other person make the decision. Some remarried persons have a very high level of friendship with former in-laws and relatives. There is no need for those relationships to die simply because of divorce or remarriage. Most of us can use all the friends we can get. If children have had good relationships with grandparents prior to your divorce, they should not be cut off from them.

Favorite aunts and uncles should not be severed from friendship because of a divorce.

Some remarrying people want to cut all the old ties and make new ones. People on the fringes of your divorce will hurt for you because of the situation. They do not need to have you hurt them back by cutting off their friendship.

Evaluate the quality of your friendships with your relatives and friends. Keep the ones that are healthy and valuable to everyone. Divorce and remarriage does not have to make you an outlaw.

HOW TO GROW TOGETHER

I have shared some thoughts in this chapter about the children, relatives, friends and ex-mates. They all make up a part of the world of the remarried. But at the center of that world are the two people who have made new vows and commitments to love, support, honor and share their lives.

Beginning again in marriage is not easy. It will take more time and patience than you ever dreamed you had. There will be a multitude of little things to be worked out each day. Things you thought you had resolved will keep coming up. You will discover some things you had not discovered prior to the marriage. There will be money problems, children problems, discipline problems, ex-mate problems, adjustment problems, legal problems and personality problems. There will be times when you may wonder what you have gotten into.

Growing a marriage is never easy, whether it is the first or second or third time around. There are always new lessons to be learned and new loves to share. The need to hang together and maintain a united effort is of extreme importance in a remarriage. There are many things that will bump into your marriage and try to steer it off course. Your commitment to one another needs to be firm and deep. If you think of jumping ship at the first sign of struggle, take a second look at your commitment and priorities.

I saw a little sign once that said, "Things are to be used, people are to be loved." It takes time to grow love. Remarriage is a genuine labor of love and it doesn't grow and bloom overnight.

PERSONAL GROWTH AND DISCUSSION QUESTIONS

1. Finish this statement: The thought of remarriage makes me feel

   Explain your response.

2. Describe how you might feel about loyalties in remarriage.

3. How do you feel about inheriting someone else's children?

4. What would be your greatest fear as a stepparent?

5. Explain how you have kept or lost relatives and friends through your divorce.

6. What three goals would you set for yourself in a remarriage.

1. _____

2. _____

3. _____

7. My personal growth goal for this week is

_____

_____

_____

_____

_____

GROWING
THROUGH
DIVORCE

11

HOW I'VE GROWN
THRU MY DIVORCE

The larger part of this book has been designed to help you walk through the various aspects of a divorce. In this chapter and the one following, a number of the members of the Positive Christian Singles of Garden Grove Community Church share how they personally have grown through their divorce. They do so with the hope that you will be inspired and challenged to grow through your divorce.

"At the time of my divorce I was 47 years old and was convinced that life didn't hold anything more for me; I lacked self-confidence, was 20 pounds overweight, couldn't speak to anyone intelligently, suffered from constant anxiety, and I was very bitter.

"I'm growing, and eventually I want to help others grow also. My education has played a big part in this growth. I've taken secretarial courses, philosophy, psychology and other significantly helpful courses at Garden Grove Community Church. Through these courses, I've learned to like myself again; I'm learning to cope with unpleasant situations, to talk to others, I've acquired new self-confidence, no longer have a problem with anxiety, bitterness or self-pity and I have inner peace and strength that I've never known before.

"The Lord works in beautiful ways when we allow him to help us grow, and I've found there's no better traveling companion through life that Jesus Christ."

RK

"Divorce was probably little different for me than for others. It was a shattering emotional experience—my world, I thought, had tumbled to the ground. I had one big party for one long year!

"I found that as I began to grow in my faith

and renew my relationship with God, that I began to find a peace within that I thought could never again come to me. I've learned that by sharing my talents, by serving and giving of myself, that God really has a plan for me. For the first time in my life, I really believe this!

"How have I grown since becoming a single? I've rediscovered life—through sharing, giving, and caring—by finding a peace within that could only come from God, by renewing my faith in God and mankind, my saying, 'God, here I am, use me as You want,' and then allowing God to work through me—His vessel, and by being a part of His plan."

JM

"After almost 21 years of marriage, my husband wanted a divorce—I thought my world had ended.

"With the messages I heard in church and Sunday School, the good friends I made, I started to grow. I found I have an identity of my own, I'm not just a Mrs. Somebody. I have a lot more growing to do, but with the help of good friends and learning more about the Lord, I will make it."

VH

"It has been said, 'You can *go* through divorce, or you can *grow* through divorce.' How true it is! Growth began with many days and nights spent in anguish and bitter tears forcing me to realize I could not expect friends or relatives to make adjustments for me. They just did not understand what I was going through. I knew I must make my own adjustments—and it was in this helpless state that I met Jesus.

"I had taken my life down many 'wrong roads,' attempting to fill a gap within myself which I know now is reserved for Christ alone. One night I prayed, 'Jesus, my life is really a mess. I'm in terrible need of some *real* understanding and love. I'm so weary of trying to figure out where everything went wrong, and carrying around this load of guilt for letting myself and so many others down. Can You just wrap Your arms around me and love me—in this state I'm in?' and He did!''

AB

"I have grown in many ways through divorce. I have learned to make decisions and be responsible for my own actions. I have more self-confidence since I have proved to myself that I can successfully work and support myself and my daughter. These things did not come about merely because I became a divorced person. I must say I prayed a lot and asked God for much guidance and direction as well as for specifics. One of those was for good friends and God answered that prayer in a very beautiful way.

"For the first time in my life, I feel good about me!"

HMD

"I truly feel I have grown through my divorce—didn't think I would ever make that statement! I'm learning to look at myself from within. I can be more honest with myself and others. Any bitterness from my marriage has been erased. I can now pray for my former mate's well-being and feel good about it. This is growth for me. God's plan for me will manifest itself—in the meantime, I'm learning, loving, and living with enthusiasm. Even little things I do have more meaning—like bending down to smell a rose on my way to work and praise God for the beauty of that flower. Gee, it's great to be me!"

PT

"How sad I felt when I chose divorce. I was not divorcing just a man, but my ownself from the world. I felt to some measure I had failed.

"I felt if I could not look back on the past without the pain and confusion that I felt, I must keep that door closed—only to open it

again when I could derive some good from it.
By closing the door to the past another opened
for me. Out of it came love—an insight into
the suffering of others—a joy of life that knows
no bounds—an understanding of myself. By
changing from an old way of life to one filled
with love and by walking with someone who
will not let you go—I have found strength. I no
longer live in darkness of a love that could not
be. For I have found completeness that has
really set me free.''

KJ

''My divorce has taught me that many people
do not appreciate a good mate. My divorce has
also led me to the Garden Grove Community
Church and Jesus. Although I've been a Jewish
Christian for over 20 years; it is only since my
association with the singles ministry that I've
really grown.''

IF

''Wow, how I've changed through divorce!
The past year has been a year of constant
adjustments and readjustment—learning and
relearning—growing, maturing and becoming
involved with God's people.''

EM

"After floundering around for a year, lonely and depressed a good deal of the time, searching for some meaning in life, I 'gave in' and asked for God's forgiveness and prayed for His love and guidance. I had tried all the other avenues, seeking happiness, so I turned to the Lord and that's when a whole new world opened up.

"I know that God has a plan for me and I know if I persevere I will one day understand. In the meantime, I'm just growing one day at a time through the love and sharing and caring with all the neat people I meet. Life is great because God is walking right beside me!"

GD

"I have grown through divorce. After having been a housewife for 23 years, cloistered in the four walls of my own home and the Women's Society of the church, etc., it was indeed a revelation to come out into the business world once again. I have developed a new tolerance for people and their actions in this world.

"Through all of this hurt, heartbreak, tears— I have called out for comfort from my God. This was something I had wanted all of my life, but it took a catastrophe like the crumbling of my marriage to bring me to actually find God. This has been the most valuable and enduring growth I have made in the last nine years, and this is such an ever growing process. There is still so much to learn—and such a long way to grow!''

PH

"When I knew I couldn't do anything to keep my marriage together any longer, I had tried everything humanly possible, I let go and let God do what He wanted to do with my life.

"I felt as if there was nothing left to live for when my husband walked out on me. But a 'still small voice' from deep within me kept me from doing something tragic.

"When I learned to put my *'total' trust* in God and let Him handle the situation, my life took on a new and different meaning. I truly believe God has a specific plan for my life if I will only let Him do the directing, which I am leaning to do. It hasn't always been easy—with ups and downs but the more I learn to put my faith and trust in Jesus Christ, each day has become easier.

"Through the Singles Group at Garden Grove Community Church, I have learned to reach out to others who have gone through the pain of divorce. GGCC Positive Christian Singles has given me a place to grow and find meaningful relationships with others.''

JM

"In Gal. 5:15 it says: But if you act like animals, hurting and harming one another, then watch out, or you will completely destroy one another.

"Here is where it all starts—the result a divorce—loneliness, despair and thoughts of suicide, if you are without God. I am a Christian and still discouragement sets in.

"However, in Romans 5:3: And we also rejoice in our troubles, because we know that trouble produces endurance, endurance brings God's approval and his approval creates hope.

"The divorced person starts to find order and the growth begins. It was hard for me to gain self-confidence and self-esteem after rejection but the Bible is full of promises and if I draw my strength from these promises what have I to really fear! The reward will be beyond your expectations. For God, through His revealed word—if you have the faith to believe—has promised amazing treasure."

CC

"Twenty-four hours after my ex-husband left for good, I suddenly became aware of the tremendous relief I felt. I looked in the mirror and saw a homely, overweight, sad eyed person with little hope for herself. Today that same person looks great and has eyes that sparkle from an inner glow. Not only do I have hope, I *know* that I am going to make it and plan to help others to do the same thing.

"If I had stayed in that unhappy marriage any longer I would have soon been no good to my children or to myself, let alone the world around us.

"Because of my faith in God, I know that someday I will meet someone that operates on the same level of communication as I do and together we can do good things for one another, our children and others not so fortunate."

SM

TEARS OF HURT AND BITTERNESS

Lord today I cannot seem to pray
or even see the way,
My heart is so full of bitterness my
clouds all turned to gray.
I know you're there, dear Lord, no matter
how the tide,
I know the Bible says you're walking
by my side.
I should not fear when Satan tempts
and makes me want to sin,
I know that's His daily job, but God,
God will help me win.
Take out the bitterness dear Lord
and all the hurt within,

Let me quit feeling sad about what
might have been.
Give me peace, and joy and happiness
instead of all the strife.
Help me to see that bitterness and
anger hurts but me,
And all my pity parties will never
have much glee.
Over and over I seem to ask the
same old question "Why?"
I know I want to give up Lord
and just lie down and die,
But in Thy plan you have a life
that's just as good for me,
Even if my tears today refuse to
let me see.
Help my faith to take on wings and
rise above this storm,
And know that when the night is
over there will be another morn!

VC

"Divorce was one of those disastrous failures that happened to other people, not to me. Until it did!

"Shock, embarrassment, shame, fear, depression, anger and denial were just a few of my chaotic reactions. To me, and up-to-my-elbows-in-anything-I-do person, my being divorced irrevocably violated a lifetime struggle to live up to God's standards. 'What now?' I asked myself. I had no answers. I asked God. He did.

"God brought new friends into my life, other Christian singles who understood because they too, had been there. They force-fed me generous servings of Christian love, which I desperately needed but refused to accept immediately! They ignored my resistance until it melted away. I was finally ready for healing.

"Many were the wounds which needed healing, yet, some seemed too painful to deal with immediately, and would have to wait. The past was too painful to dwell on and the future was too scary, lonely, and unknown to plan for. I was stuck with just living one day at a time. I tried to handle each problem as it occurred rather than hoarding it with other similar problems from the past. It was kind of neat!

"Not surprisingly, I began to enjoy life more and felt my confidence returning. Somehow, that was hard to accept. I mean, I was divorced! Didn't that mean miserable! What if I began to enjoy being single! I might never know love again! Horrible thought! 'Hey!' God gently reminded me. 'Leave the future to Me!' 'Okay, Lord.'

"A *lifetime* of loneliness I cannot face. But a *day* alone had some harmlessly selfish pleasures, I found. Little things, really, but nice.

"Although it's been up and down, He has been faithful. I've learned that married isn't *better* for all its wonderful intimacy where two people can share more with a private joke or significant look than most people with a thousand words. I've learned that single isn't *better* for all its freedom to be. I've learned that NOW is *better*, for it's my chance to grow, to be alive!

"*Now* I will be content. I will squeeze in as close as I can to God—lean, cry, laugh and grow through Him. He has promised to strengthen my inner person as I seek to know and understand Him. Things are great, and getting better!"

BR

"We were three hurting people; a husband, a wife, and a 6-year old son. The divorce opened the way to growth for each of us."

GS

"The step of faith and total dependence upon God for direction regarding my divorce eleven years ago, was only the beginning of a series of traumatic spiritual and emotional growth episodes for me. Why God would allow something which seemed contrary to all of my beliefs and training was a fact which I could not comprehend, however, the peace and assurance which I was given, provided the strength to endure pain and turmoil such as I had never thought possible. Now I know personally, that God leads us in ways which we do not understand. I am learning through my experiences how to better relate to others with a new dimension of love, acceptance and understanding and appreciation. My life has new meaning and purpose, and I find myself willingly giving of my time and energy to help others grow emotionally and spiritually also.

"Sharing love and understanding with others is a very special ministry. My outlook has gone from very narrow to that of wearing wide-angle lenses."

PMK

"After our divorce, I did well to live from day to day. Now my children and I have a much better relationship than we have ever had, because we are growing. We are much more honest with each other, considerate and tolerant of each other's ideas and life-styles. The love we feel for each other is much easier for us to express than it was in the past. It's wonderful to feel the love and encouragement of your children.

"For the first time in my life my relationship with God is something I want to share. I have met some really great people at work through this sharing.

My kids listen to a folk singer, John Stewart, who sings something that seems to express the way I need to live to grow in this world, 'You can't look back; you just got to keep movin' on.' May the good Lord always help me to keep moving on!"

LM

"I was married three times in the past twenty-four years—to make it short, the change brought about by divorce is my finding and accepting Jesus Christ. While I can't know exactly what Christ has planned as each day goes by things become a little clearer. As I've heard said many times, when you need more light on your path, Christ will provide. All I must remember is that I'm no longer in charge."

JW

"Two and a half years after our marriage we separated and a year later divorced. It was the first time I had lost someone or something I wanted. I blamed myself for most of our problems.

"I tried unsuccessfully to find identity in bars and other people. I'm growing and loving today because of my relationship with God, myself and others."

EB

HOW HAVE YOU GROWN THROUGH YOUR DIVORCE? I invite you to take a few moments and pencil or pen in some of your own growth experiences to make this chapter complete. You will be joining with some of God's beautiful people in your sharing. And you will be helping in the writing of this book and in your own growth process.

_____

_____

_____

_____

_____

_____

_____

GROWING THROUGH DIVORCE

12

HOW I'VE GROWN IN MY REMARRIAGE

"Growing in remarriage is only possible for me when I have the *freedom* to do so. This freedom comes through prayer—surrendering what I cannot handle. Important to keep a balance at all times, Christ, myself and others. (Others in order of priority: husband, children, parent-relatives, employment.)

"Ultimate goal is to take the personal out of situations of stress and see the issue at the bottom, i.e. children, stepchildren, in-laws, ex-mates. By taking the personal out, I can then examine issues, situations, and make decisions with the *freedom* and desire.

"Psychology is great, the different techniques helpful in relieving your anxieties—guilt, etc. but they all fail in the final test—all but Jesus Christ who through my personal test has met me wherever I am and forgiven me any and all transgressions—he is freedom personified. Freedom to be, and grow each day of our lives."

KF

"I consider myself a very lucky man, God has blessed me and I know that he is the source of my happiness. Whenever we have minor problems, it never fails that we have taken Christ out of the center of our marriage. It is then we realize that through God we can be happy and grow in our marriage. It is then we realize that through God we can be happy and grow in our marriage and Christian life. I am truly grateful to Him for all He has given me."

TF

"Having gone through the pain and agony of a divorce, my wife and I seem to understand each other and appreciate each other more.

"After my brief bout with alcoholism, we gave our lives to the Lord. This has both enriched and enhanced our marriage. God has been very good to us and has blessed our family and our marriage. We would heartily recommend remarriage to anyone considering it and would offer the following advise that we consider has helped to make our marriage a success: Base your marriage ON—THRU—AND IN GOD. Seek His help and guidance in all that you do."

RS & BS

"Five months before we were married, we walked to the altar at Garden Grove Community Church and re-dedicated our lives to God. Like so many others who were raised in a Christain home, we were always so near the forest we failed to see or really know the One who made it all possible.

"Now we are married and not only have a close relationship with each other, but one that can never be broken—because God is the hub of our life."

GD & JD

"The entrance into remarriage as 'older and wiser adults' having chosen, if not the ideal, the more nearly ideal mate often lends itself to irony. We find we face many of the same hassles and, with children already on the scene, some new conflicts.

"The promoter of growth in our marriage is called 'communication.' An all-inclusive word that delves into many facets. Fortunately, we recognize the need for it and keep striving to achieve open, concerned, sincere communication.

"Above all, our verbal communication of 'I love you' and our knowledge of our love through Jesus Christ has sustained us and enhanced our marriage."

JI & GI

"We feel that the most important concept in remarriage is a common goal. Ours is to reach for the Lord. Also, the time spent each week sharing with other Christian remarrieds, has strengthened our relationship. The sharing of their solutions to problems as well as their joys, has helped us gain insight to problems which arise in our own situation. Through all this we have gained the freedom to allow each other to grow toward the individual the Lord means for us to be."

BW & SW

"After my divorce, a big adjustment was to become independent—which meant to stand alone and make decisions for myself. After I remarried, my biggest adjustment was to relearn to consider someone else in my decisions and actions.

"Remarriage has heightened my awareness of myself in relation to others. Not only my husband but also my dealings regarding his former wife. It seemed a lot easier to apply my interpretation of the golden rule to everyone in the entire world—except his former wife. I am learning to make decisions regarding his ex from more of an objective viewpoint regarding her as a person and not as a threat.

"Remarriage has expanded my family! I now have six children instead of two. Four of them visit for weekends twice each month; but we do a lot of planning and preparation for their visits to provide 'real' family emphasis.

"We are daily learning to mesh our personalities to enhance the better qualities in each of us."

ES

"You cannot be happy with someone unless you are happy with yourself—this means you cannot let the past make you unhappy.

"It is very important to keep the lines of

communication open at all times. You will grow in love because communication and love grow together. Love is something that does not grow by itself, you have to work at it.

"Do not make children your first consideration, so your mate will not be a stranger to you. You can help your children more by setting an example of a good Christian marriage. Make God the head of your home."

GC

A NUMBER OF PEOPLE EXPRESS
THEIR GROWTH IN REMARRIAGE
IN THE FOLLOWING WAYS:

"Have learned to be more patient and understanding about some things that I have taken for granted."

"I have grown within myself and my relationship with my husband by having complete communication."

"Some similar problems as in the first marriage develop—however, in the second marriage each has learned how to better deal with them and how better to communicate our feelings."

"The Lord has given me greater insight into the feelings of my partner and to show appreciation for his many good points."

"More willing to openly discuss areas that bother me about my job, friends, spouse, etc. More secure and positive about myself and goals."

GROWING
THROUGH
DIVORCE

13

HOW TO KEEP THE SCALES
OF JUSTICE FROM TILTING

"Why do I need an attorney?"

Divorce is the death of a marriage and is usually surrounded by a cast of players that includes the husband and wife as combatants, the children as the mourners, and the lawyers as the funeral directors.

Lawyers are often maligned for the role they play in the divorce cases in our society. Some look upon them as eager vultures in search of big fees. Others look to them as friends and guides in this strange land called Divorce Country. They know the bends in the road, the potholes, the construction areas, the danger zones, the dead ends. They are often thrust into the roles of social worker, counselor, therapist, priest and doctor. A good lawyer will not forget to put his humanity and love for people alongside his law books and court presentations.

One of the first questions I ask a person who announces they are contemplating or are in the process of divorce is, "Have you obtained an attorney and consulted with him?" I am amazed at how many people leave this decision up to someone else or just don't think of it at all. Many who do not want a divorce respond by saying, "Why do I need an attorney?"

One of the most important things to remember, whether you want the divorce or not, is GET AN ATTORNEY RIGHT AWAY! A good divorce attorney can make a world of difference in helping you walk through all the legal implications that divorce imposes.

I meet people every day who were tricked, conned, and hoodwinked into losing literally everything in their divorce because they did not secure a good attorney in time. If one mate has a competent attorney and the other does not, it may mean the difference in a good settlement or a bad one.

WHERE DO YOU FIND A GOOD ATTORNEY?

Most attorneys come through personal recommendation of friends or relatives. They should not come through leafing through the yellow pages of your telephone book. A telephone call to the local bar association can often be beneficial in helping you find a lawyer who specializes in divorce cases. You do need an attorney who is an expert in the divorce field rather than one who maybe handles three or four cases a year. Laws continue to change and those who specialize in certain areas tend to keep up to date on the changes that affect their field. A good question of inquiry to an attorney would be, "What percentage of your cases each year deal with divorce?" If the percentage is high, it could indicate that the attorney specializes in this area. Don't be afraid to ask questions. Find out what you need to know before you hire legal counsel.

SOME HELPFUL HINTS FROM AN ATTORNEY

I have asked an attorney friend of mine who specializes in divorce proceedings to share some of his wisdom with you. Here are his suggestions:

1. Exhaust all reasonable joint efforts in seeking competent family counseling before seeking divorce.
   a) Singular efforts of one spouse seldom results in joint insight into the problems and solutions that can keep a marriage together.
   b) Carefully select a counselor through trusted sources of referral or recommendation.
   c) Approach all counseling with an open mind. At worst you might get a new look at "the real you."
2. If there is a basis to believe one party will abscond with or dissipate liquid assets (joint bank accounts, etc.), freeze these assets (by removal to singular bank accounts, etc.)
   a) This is not considered improper. Such action simply preserves the estate for future disposition (payment of debts, equal division of community property, attorney fees, etc.)

b) No unfair advantage is gained. The court can require you to account for these assets at a later date, which you should be able and willing to do.

3. Avoid the "Do It Yourself" divorce (now called dissolution in California) unless there is little or no assets and no issues of child or spousal support (alimony).

4. Discussions of settlements with your spouse's attorney may be acceptable, but *NEVER* enter into any final agreement until you at least consult with counsel of your own choosing.
   a) Conserving attorney's fees is commendable but not at the cost of your unending regret.
   b) Do not be lulled into the belief that one attorney can represent both parties. If in doubt, ask the attorney who his client really is.

5. If litigation ensues, select your attorney carefully.
   a) Again, seek your attorney through a trusted source of referral. Changing horses in mid-stream can be expensive.

6. Personally evaluate your attorney (Oh yes you can!)
   a) Ask him pointed questions (evaluate the directness and logic of his answers):
      - Length of time in practice
      - Experience in the field of domestic relations
      - Anticipated fees and costs
      - How he intends to approach his task
   b) Do not always expect concrete definitive answers at the first conference as they are seldom possible. In fact, be wary of "guarantees."
   c) Have a firm understanding with him? Do you feel you have a rapport?

7. Have a firm understanding with your attorney as to his fees from the outset.
   a) It is your right to know. (When is the last time you made a major purchase without first asking the price?)
   b) Beware the attorney that is resentful to questions about his fees. (You can't afford him, in more ways than you know.)
8. Feel free at all times to frankly discuss the problems and to ask questions of your attorney.
   a) Don't complain about not getting answers if you never asked.
   b) Never lie to your attorney (or doctor or minister).
   c) Listen and act on his advice. That's what you are paying for.
9. Communicate your fears and desires to your attorney.
   a) Although results cannot be guaranteed, it is only in this fashion that your attorney can attempt to get the desired results in the end.
10. *Live with the results.* Vindictiveness leads to destruction. Learn from yesterday and prepare for tomorrow.

These are basic hints that will help you to work with your attorney. Some practical things that can be added to this list from my personal experience are:
1. Remember that legal proceedings take time. Courts have great backlogs of cases. Yours is not the only one before them. Many divorce proceedings can go on for several years, depending upon the involvements.
2. Don't call your lawyer every day about the irrelevant and mundane things that you are going through. His work is

legal. A good counselor or therapist can help you in the non-legal things.

3. Don't sign any papers or make any agreements with an ex-spouse without consulting your lawyer.
4. Let your lawyer speak for you in legal matters.
5. Remember that in the heat of personal emotional conflict in divorce, the coolest head on your side may be your attorney. Listen to his wisdom and clear thinking.
6. Divorce laws in our country are changing rapidly. They vary from state to state. Don't assume that something you heard from another state is true in yours.
7. Don't take legal advice from your friends who have gone through a divorce. Every situation is unique in itself and there are too many variables to assume that you can do what someone else did or that your end results will be the same as theirs.

The legal involvements of divorce are seldom easy. Someone has said that anyone experiencing divorce needs three things: a good friend, a good attorney and God!

PERSONAL GROWTH AND
GROUP DISCUSSION QUESTIONS

1. Did you have your own attorney during your divorce?

2. What kind of job did he do in your behalf?

3. Do you feel you received fair treatment in the legal aspects of your divorce settlement?

4. Describe what you learned from the legal aspects of your divorce.

5. How would you change any of the current divorce laws in your state?

6. Were your legal settlements simple or complex? Explain if you can without being too personal.

7. My personal growth goal for this week is

_____

_____

_____

_____

_____

GROWING
THROUGH
DIVORCE

14

HOW TO HELP OTHERS
GROW THROUGH DIVORCE

"It seems like everyone I meet is getting divorced."

Depending on what statistics you believe, the divorce rate is either going up or coming down. There is no one reason for the great number of divorces in our society. Every divorce is different and every set of circumstances has its own variables.

We are living in an age of dramatic cultural changes. Traditions, trends, styles, feelings, and attitudes seem to change each time the daily newspaper is published. Values that were held sacred and ideal seem to have vanished into history. Our mobile way of life in both career and daily life-style has caused a rootlessness in our families. The concept of a "use and discard" society has crept into the feelings we have about people. A person is used and replaced without much thought of how they will be affected. People are discarded in industry and in marriage with about as much concern as we have in throwing our pop bottles in the garbage. Our "people-attitudes" become confused with our "merchandising-attitudes." If something or someone doesn't work, we throw it away and get a new one. New freedoms and feelings brought about by the women's movement have had a dramatic influence on our changing culture. Man's quest to get in touch with himself and raise his own consciousness level has dramatically influenced contemporary attitudes on many things. However, people will continue to marry and divorce for whatever reasons they can think up.

In a recent conversation, a person said, "It seems like everyone I meet is getting divorced." Somehow when we go through crises in our life, we become very aware of others around us who are experiencing the same thing. It is easy to attract those who can commiserate with you in your dilemma. It happens if you break your leg, wreck your car, lose your appendix or leave your marriage. Experience is valuable and it teaches us many things. One of the good things about it is that we can share what we learn with others. After growing through your own divorce, you will have something very valuable to pass along to others. Here are several guidelines that will enable you to help others who are getting divorced.

DON'T JUDGE

When two people decide to divorce, it usually sets the stage for battle lines to be drawn among the immediate family and friends. People will choose the team they want to support and then begin the process of pronouncing judgements on the other party. Families and friendships are torn to shreds because people refuse to remain neutral and try to be a friend to both divorcing parties. Sometimes people are pushed into taking sides by the separating people themselves. They might not be granted the privilege of neutrality.

In every divorce there are endless entanglements that outsiders should seek to avoid. Express to both divorcing parties that you appreciate each of them as persons and your friendship with them is not based upon their personal performance with each other. Ask them to let you remain neutral and continue your friendship with each as you choose. When family or friends try to induce you to take sides, tell them you are not qualified to be either lawyer or judge in the situation and that you choose to make decisions for yourself.

LISTEN WITH LOVE AND UNDERSTANDING

A good counselor is always a good listener. A good friend can be both counselor and listener to a person moving into a divorce Most people do not need answers. They need people who will listen to them in love and understanding. And listening takes time and patience. It is hearing people out. Letting them vent their feelings, frustrations and hostilities. It is trying to understand where they are coming from in their life.

You can help a divorcing friend by offering to listen to them whenever they need it. The first months after the initial separation can be the loneliest and hardest. Good friends who will listen are valuable. And remember that listening with love means refusing to draw judgements.

BE SUPPORTIVE IN ANY WAY YOU CAN

A popular song a few years ago contained the lines, "Just call me brother if you need a hand. We all need somebody to lean on." We have all had the experience of needing help and support from another person in difficult times. Another song proclaims that "no man is an island, no man can stand alone." A divorcing person needs a group of people around them who can help them in the human and practical ways. It may mean helping them move, having a garage sale, finding a new job, arranging babysitting, finding a lawyer, etc. Doing everything alone in post divorce adjustment can be frightening and emotionally draining. Having a corps of friends who can assist where needed is encouraging. Asking the simple question, "How can I help?" will convey your supportiveness.

GIVE DIRECTION WHERE YOU CAN

Advice is cheap. We all have an opinion on everything under the sun. But getting good directions from other people is sometimes very difficult. Giving good directions is even tougher. What we learn by our own experience does not make us an authority on the subject but it may give us something valuable to pass along to someone else. Know your limitations on giving help and direction to other people. Help where you feel comfortable and where you can.

REFER PEOPLE TO AVAILABLE RESOURCES

Every community has an endless list of human resources. Most people are totally unaware that they even exist simply because they have never needed them The first resource that a person going through a divorce needs is a competent lawyer. Others might be a social worker, a job counselor, a professional therapist or counselor.

Many people who have gone through a divorce can recommend some very competent assistance to those entering the experience. There are many Divorce Recovery and Rehabilitation Seminars that are offered by colleges, universities and counseling agencies. They all have different names but all seek to help a person through the entire process of divorce. One of the by-products of this kind of workshop is that you meet and share with other people like yourself. New friendships are made and new growth takes place.

Another unused and overlooked resource is the public library. There are numerous good books that will enlighten and assist the divorcing person. A short bibliography is found at the back of this book.

A divorced person is in the process of making a transition from one way of living to another. It is a difficult process and one that requires a great deal of help and patience. If you have experienced divorce in your own life, you can be a great help to someone else by sharing some of the things in this chapter and some of the things you have personally learned.

**GROWING
THROUGH
DIVORCE**

15

GROWING THROUGH DIVORCE

A SUMMARY

YOU CAN GO THROUGH IT.......OR GROW THROUGH IT!

This is the thought that we have been sharing with you throughout this book. You can become a battered, bruised and bitter statistic like so many thousands of divorced persons today, or you can let your divorce be a growth producing experience in your life. You can use it to build a better YOU and a better life for you.

We have not intimated anywhere in this book that divorce is an easy process and to be treated lightly. It is a hard, cold, emotion wrenching experience that can devastate a human being. It is probably one of the least understood and most ignored social problems of our time. Little understanding and less help is available to those caught in divorce.

We have shared in these pages some practical insights and guidelines that can help you turn your divorce into a growth experience. We have offered no easy solutions, no magical cures, no philosophizing. We have said that divorce hurts and it does. It takes time and hard work to heal the hurts. There will be some days when you will feel so low that you will have to reach up to touch bottom. There will be other days when you will feel that the battle is won. You will have good days and bad days.

I encourage you to put the principles and suggestions from this book into practice in your life. *You have to do the work*. The book will not do it for you.

I want to leave you with these words of hope, written by the Apostle Paul to some early struggling Christians:

> "We are afflicted in every way,
> but not crushed;
> perplexed but not despairing,
> persecuted but not forsaken,
> struck down but not destroyed."
>   (II Cor. 4:8 & 9)

TEN COMMANDMENTS FOR FORMERLY MARRIEDS

1. THOU SHALT NOT LIVE IN THY PAST.

2. THOU SHALT BE RESPONSIBLE FOR THY PRESENT AND NOT BLAME THY PAST FOR IT.

3. THOU SHALT NOT FEEL SORRY FOR THYSELF INDEFINITELY.

4. THOU SHALT ASSUME THY END OF THE BLAME FOR THY MARRIAGE DISSOLVEMENT.

5. THOU SHALT NOT TRY TO RECONCILE THY PAST AND RECONSTRUCT THY FUTURE BY A QUICK, NEW MARRIAGE.

6. THOU SHALT NOT MAKE THY CHILDREN THE VICTIMS OF THY PAST MARRIAGE.

7. THOU SHALT NOT SPEND ALL THY TIME TRYING TO CONVINCE THY CHILDREN HOW TERRIBLE AND EVIL THEIR DEPARTED PARENT IS.

8. THOU SHALT LEARN ALL THOU CAN ABOUT BEING A ONE PARENT FAMILY AND GET ON WITH IT.

9. THOU SHALT ASK OTHERS FOR HELP WHEN THOU NEEDEST IT.

10. THOU SHALT ASK GOD FOR THE WISDOM TO BURY YESTERDAY, CREATE TODAY AND PLAN FOR TOMORROW.

**GROWING
THROUGH
DIVORCE**

BIBLIOGRAPHY OF
RESOURCE BOOKS

Addeo, Edmond and Burger, Robert. *Inside Divorce*, Chilton, 1975

Baer, Jean. *The Second Wife*, Doubleday

Becker, Russell J. *When Marriage Ends*, Fortress Press, 1971

Bernard, Jesse. *Remarriage: A Study of Marriage*, Russell & Russell, 1956

Bohannon, Paul *Divorce and After*, Doubleday

Champagne, Marian. *Facing Life Alone*, Bobbs Merrill

Edwards, Marie and Hoover, Eleanor. *The Challenge of Being Single*, Hawthorne-Tarch, 1974

Egleson, Janet and Jim. *Parents Without Partners*, E. O. Dutton, 1961

Epstein, Joseph. *Divorced in America*, E. P. Dutton, 1974

Fisher, Esther. *Divorce, the New Freedom*, Harper & Row

Gardner, Richard A. *The Boys and Girls Book About Divorce*, Bantam, 1970

Gettlemen, Susan & Markowitz, Janet. *The Courage to Divorce*, Ballantine, 1974

Hallett, Kathryn. *People in Crisis*, Celestial Arts, 1974

Hope, Carol and Young, Nancy. *Momma: The Sourcebook for Single Mothers,* Plume Books, 1976

Hosier, Helen. *The Other Side of Divorce*, Hawthorne, 1975

Hudson, R. Loften. *Till Divorce Do Us Part*, Nelson Press, 1973

Drantzler, Mel. *Creative Divorce*, M. Evans & Co., 1973

Maddox, Brenda. *The Half Parent*, M. Evans & Co., 1975

Ramsey, James. ''Who Am I Now That I Am Alone,'' (Group discussion series available from James Ramsey, 13222 E. Bailey St., Whittier, Ca. 90601)

Schuller, Robert H. *You Can Become The Person You Were Meant To Be*, Hawthorne, 1973

Schuller, Robert H. *Self Love*, Hawthorne, 1969

Schuller, Robert H. *Move Ahead With Possibility Thinking*, Doubleday, 1967

Small, Dwight. *The Right to Remarry,* Revell, 1975

Stewart, Suzanne. *Divorced, I Wouldn't Have Given You a Nickel for Your Chances*, Zondervan, 1974

Taves, Isabella. *Woman Alone*, Funk and Wagnalls

Weiss, Robert S. *Loneliness*, M.I.T. Press, 1973

Weiss, Robert S. *Marital Separation*, Basic Books, 1976

GROWING
THROUGH
DIVORCE

NOTES

NOTES

NOTES

NOTES

NOTES

NOTES